DIARY FOR 1851
OF
JOHN MUNRO MACKENZIE
CHAMBERLAIN
OF THE LEWS
TO
SIR JAMES MATHESON

The publishers extend their appreciation to J.H.M. MacKenzie, the Diarist's great-grandson, for permission to publish this Diary, and for access to the documents and photographs reproduced there-in.

"The Laying of the Foundation Stone of Lews Castle," and the key to the painting from the Annals of Lodge Fortrose No 108, Stornoway, 1767-1905, are reproduced by kind permission of Lodge Fortrose No 108, Stornoway.

The Publisher acknowledges subsidy from the Scottish Arts Council towards the publication of this volume.

We are particularly grateful to Sheila MacLeod for her transcription, and to James Shaw Grant for writing the Foreword.

First published in Scotland in 1994 by Acair Ltd,
7 James Street, Stornoway, Isle of Lewis

Designed by Acair Ltd.
Cover illustration by Andrew MacMorran
Printed by Highland Printers, Inverness

ISBN 0 86152 908 1 (Hardback)
ISBN 0 86152 923 5 (Paperback)

Diary

1851

John Munro Mackenzie

Chamberlain of the Lews

acair

Contents

The Diary is printed in a format which follows as faithfully as possible the author's original manuscript. Deviations from accepted orthography, omissions or slips of the pen, are indicated in italics within parentheses.

Foreword

On New Year's day, 1851, John Munro Mackenzie, the Chamberlain and Baron Bailie of Lewis, deviated from his normal routine and thereby put us deeply in his debt. New Year's Day was not then a public holiday, nor was Christmas Day: the Chamberlain was in his office on both, and New Year's Day was particularly busy because it was the traditional day for settling debts. The deviation, which is so important to us, came at the end of the day, when the Chamberlain opened a diary and recorded all that he had done.

It is not a diary in the usual sense of the term. The Chamberlain was not communing with himself. There is nothing self-regarding or introspective in the record he kept. His *Diary* is a brief, factual note of where he went, whom he saw and what he did. It is more of a time sheet than a personal diary. One wonders why he kept it at all, and, having kept it, restricted it to precisely one year.

It may have been the basis for his periodic reports to his rather exacting employer, Sir James Matheson Bart, who had amassed a fortune in China, as one of the co-founders of Jardine Matheson and Company, trading, as their critics said, with the Bible in one hand and opium in the other. Or it may have simply been the decision of a shrewd business man, that he should have a careful record of events throughout a year, which he knew, even before it began, would be difficult, because of the policy his employer had decided to pursue.

The Chamberlain's great-grandson, J. H. M. Mackenzie, renewed the family association with Lewis, when he became owner of one of the leading firms in the Harris Tweed industry, and proprietor of Scaliscro Estate. Recognising the historical importance of the *Diary*, he has now made it available for publication.

The estate John Munro Mackenzie administered extended to more than 400,000 acres, with a population just short of 20,000, mostly Gaelic-speaking crofters, living in more than a hundred villages, all but three of them on the coast. He was responsible for fixing and collecting the rents; settling disputes between tenants; developing and maintaining the road system, such as it was; organising transport to and from the mainland through the packet boat provided by his employer; administering the Poor Law through four parish committees; and supervising the schools. There was no aspect of the life of the community in which he was not, under Sir James, the ultimate authority, or the prime mover, or, at least, the most important influence. There were even occasions when he was called on, as a sort of court of appeal, to review decisions he had taken himself in another capacity, and it must be said, to his credit, that he sometimes reversed his own earlier judgement.

Even in a normal year the responsibilities of the Chamberlain of Lewis were immense and a record of his activities would be of interest for that alone. The value of the document is, however, increased immeasurably because 1851 was a climactic year in the island's history. Before John Munro Mackenzie became Chamberlain, Lewis had suffered the hardships of the Hungry Forties. The sufferings had been less intense than they might have been, because Sir James Matheson had bought meal to avert starvation. The *Diary*, on one of its early pages, records the award of a baronetcy to him in public recognition of his generosity. The generosity, however, was less than appeared on the surface. Mackenzie's predecessor, with or without Sir James's instruction, had charged up the meal to the crofters' rent. The vast arrears which the years of failed harvests had inevitably created, were thus swollen quite unmanageably and the whole economy of the island was threatening to break down: many crofters who could, by 1851, afford to pay their rents, were reluctant to do so, because many others seemed to be going scot free. In addition to the problems created by the famine years, the population of Lewis was growing from 16% to 21%, decade after decade. That in itself created serious tensions in an island where the whole economy rested, or was assumed to rest, on the occupation of land. The problem facing the Chamberlain as he grappled with the situation he inherited from his predecessor was greatly increased by a disagreement between him and his employer on a fundamental issue. The Chamberlain saw the active development of the fishing industry as one way of alleviating the economic problems of the island. The Proprietor, while pursuing a grandiose scheme to make paraffin from peat, thought the development of the fishing industry should be left to the free play of market forces. He did not explain how the enterprise of other people could create the necessary infrastructure, in an island where every inch of land was owned by himself.

Sir James's policy was relatively simple in economic terms. He wanted to get rid of those who were irretrievably in arrears with their rent, and re-let the land to those who could pay. The surplus population was not to be evicted in the Sutherland style by burning the thatch and letting them fend for themselves. They were to be given the alternative of emigrating to Canada, on ships which he was chartering, to re-settle in locations which he had pre-arranged, and accompanied by a Free Church minister, for their spiritual consolation, whom he proposed to recruit. John Munro Mackenzie had the unenviable task of selecting those who were to emigrate, re-letting the land to those who remained, organising the ships on which the emigrants were to sail, and recovering in the process, as much of the rent arrears as he could.

The *Diary* is like the record of one side of a mammoth game of chess, with real men and women as pieces on the board: we know every move made by White, the opening player, but we can only deduce the responses of Black from the abundant folk-memories the events of 1851 left in their wake. The most remarkable fact, having regard to what was happening elsewhere in the Highlands, in similar circumstances, at the same time, is that the mass exodus from Lewis was carried through without the intervention of a single soldier or policeman, and with no civil disobedience of any sort.

The explanation lies largely in the terms that were offered. However they appear to us today, they provided the emigrants of 1851 with an escape from an intolerable situation. The fact that John Munro Mackenzie was himself a Lewisman, no doubt also helped. Most of those who held the post of Chamberlain, both before him and after him, were incomers who had little sympathy with the local people, and sometimes openly despised them. John Munro Mackenzie, however, was born in Stornoway, according to family tradition, and certainly spent much of his youth in Lewis. His father was for many years the Island's Sheriff. One of his grandfathers was an Island minister. A paternal uncle, Murdoch Mackenzie, and a maternal uncle, John Munro, were lieutenants in the 78th Highlanders, and took part, with hundreds of Lewismen, in Wellington's memorable victory at Assaye. Both lost their lives in the Far East and John Munro Mackenzie, when he was Chamberlain, used to seek out their surviving comrades to hear their stories of events in which his uncles had taken part. He also obtained, belatedly, for the survivors campaign medals, although by that time few of them were fit to attend the parade at which they were presented.

John Munro Mackenzie also seems to have been a man of some sensitivity. When he set off from Stornoway for his first job in

Glasgow he carried a testimonial from the local minister, Rev. John Cameron, which described him as "a young gentleman of an amiable disposition, genteel in his manner, affable in his conversation and mild in his disposition". A testimonial, written by a family friend on such an occasion, must be read with some reserve, but the impression it gives of the man receives some confirmation from a paper he wrote in 1851, in which he tries to convince himself that the emigration was not compulsory. The argument is unconvincing, but the mere fact that he had qualms about the matter distinguishes him dramatically from his successor, the notorious Donald Munro, and from most of the predecessors of whom we have record.

One of the most important visitors to Lewis, in the year covered by the *Diary*, was Sir John MacNeill, Chairman of the Board of Supervision for Poor Relief in Scotland. Sir John was an even stronger advocate of emigration, as the solution to the Highland problem, than Sir James Matheson, and the rules of the Board of Supervision bore more heavily on the poor than the practice of the Lewis estate under John Munro Mackenzie. It must give us pause, as we read the *Diary*, to think that the crofters were better off, under the regime the Chamberlain was reporting on than they would have been under the direct "care" and "protection" of the British government. Security of tenure was still a full generation in the future, and even when the crofters had security, out-migration continued unabated for nearly half a century, and still continues to a lesser extent, and in a highly selective way.

Sir John, in his report on the Hebridean crofters, comments on "the tenacity of their attachment to their native soil," citing the case of a man from Waternish, in Skye, who for twenty successive years, migrated to the Lothians and worked for six months on a farm, in order "that he might continue to enjoy his croft and comparative idleness for the other half year in Waternish." Sir John, and the historians who have since quoted from his report, regard this attachment to the land as an eccentricity, almost an absurdity, and a barrier to progress. They have not stopped to enquire whether it is really an attachment to the land, or something much more fundamental: a recognition that human beings are social rather than economic animals, and that the dominant culture in a state is not necessarily the best. That argument is still very much alive in post-Thatcherite Britain, and is probably more urgent now than it was when Sir John MacNeill sat down with John Munro Mackenzie to discuss it, over a bottle of wine, in Lews Castle, in 1851.

10

As for the emigrants, they went to Lower Quebec and Bruce County in Ontario. The community established in Lower Quebec has now disappeared, largely because of the pressure of the French-Canadian culture which surrounded it. However there is still an identifiable community in Bruce County. They are now Canadians, not Scots, but they know their history. The same is true of many of the Bruce County settlers who later moved further west into the prairies. In recent years their ties with Lewis have been strengthened, through the activities of Bill Lawson of the Genealogical Centre in Northton, Harris. From time to time descendants of the 1851 emigrants return to Lewis to seek their roots, including Elizabeth Ogilvie, the American novelist, one of whose stories, "The Silent Ones", is based on the experiences of a writer who "came home".

John Munro Mackenzie, after leaving Lewis, was involved in business in Cumberland, and in the Lowlands of Scotland. Eventually he became proprietor of the Mornish Estate on the Island of Mull. He was visited there by Col Macleod of Drynoch, whose sister was married to Hugh Munro Mackenzie, the Chamberlain's brother. Col Macleod, at the time of the visit, was on his way to Canada, and he named one of the great Canadian cities, Calgary, founded in 1883, after the Chamberlain's home.

James Shaw Grant
Inverness
January 1994

Wednesday 1 Jan'y 1851 —
to office and was engaged settling
a/cts with Mr McPherson Galson and
giving his rent for last year — Settled
a/ct with Mr Gerrie Coultill —
sy various parties visit the Bunker
aston Country people — Going over
d A/c — led a/c — Store A/c making
gements for balancing Same — Going
paying salaries + writing letters to
ous parties —

        Thursday 2 Jan'y
fice Meeting with people to pay rents,
ing letters to various parties — Going
accounts — Went to Guinsha der
spect Work doing by Houston Hog
& on line of ring fence, + agreed
them to trench various pieces of
nd requiring it at £5 & 10/ per acre.
t to land improving + houses built
... & people Contracted with

Wednesday 1 Jany 1851

Went to office and was engaged settling accounts with Mr McPherson Galson and arranging his rent for last year. Settled for rent with Mr Gerrie Goathill. Meeting various parties, vizt the Banker, Mr Houston, country people — Going over rental a/cs — Seed a/cs — At Store a/c making arrangements for balancing same — going over a/c & paying salaries etc. Writing letters to various parties —

Thursday 2nd Jan^y

At office meeting with people to pay rents, writing letters to various parties — going over accounts. Went to Guirshader to inspect work doing by Houston & Co^y. Fixed on line of ring fence & agreed with them to trench various pieces of ground requiring it at £5.10/- per acre. Went to land improving & houses built by Bayhead people, Contracted with John McIver and John McLean Masons to build four houses for poor widows @ £7.10/- each — Went to Goathill & arranged with Mr Ritchie & Gerrie how the Carse land was to be sub divided and drained by open ditches — Sent David McIntosh formerly foreman at Uig to manage at Holm & Sand^k Hill at a salary of £35 per annum with a Cows Grass — Arranged with Mr Cameron about lotting Holm, Lower Sandwick & Laxdale —

Friday 3 Jany 1851

Went to the office, and was engaged writing letters — and giving tickets to members of Fishermens Society — Went over Plans and Specification of Terrace wall, & advertised same for contractors — Went to Melbost to see work doing in repairing Roads by Statute labour. Proceeded to Aignes to arrange with Mr Alexander about repairs required at his Steading, spent a considerable time with him in endeavouring to arrange matters, but Alex^r being rather drunk we separated without coming to any conclusion, he saying he would leave at next term rather than stand to the bargain made at our former meeting — The Steading cannot be put into any state of proper repair under £300 — I do not think it would be any great loss should Alexander leave, he is such an untidy farmer & never in his sober senses — Went to Garrabost & inspected the Tile Work which seems to be doing well at present — Proceeded to Bayble to see work doing on Crofts, the people are more anxious than ever to work now, as we are wishing to Stop them —

Saturday 4 Jan^y

Went to office and was engaged writing letters — Going over rentals of Parishes of Uig & Stornoway — Auditing accounts of Water Co^y, went over the whole a/cs since the Commencement — Going over the cash a/c for last year — Packet arrived received letters from Mr Matheson & Mr Souter etc

Monday 6 Jan^y

Went to office and was occupied there all day writing letters for Packet — Making up abstract of last years receipts & expenditure, the former amounting to £13955.14/9 and the latter to £25932.12/6. Wrote Mr Matheson and Mr Souter on the subject of it.

Tuesday 7 Jan^y

At office meeting parties Mr N McIver, Bowie etc Writing letters — Went to Callanish to attend meeting of Uig poor law Board accompanied by Mr M McAulay — Met Mr Ross the Stornoway Inspector at Callanish & with him went over Draft of Mr McRaes Memorial to the Gov^t making certain alterations & additions. Submitted same to the Parochial Board when the Chairman was authorised to sign it in name of the meeting. All the members of the Board seemed favourable to emigration — Went over the Collector's a/cs — Both Collector and Inspector were ordered to place their books & a/cs in the hands of Messrs M McAulay & J M MacKenzie who were appointed to audit the same — arranged various matters with the Ground Officer — Did not get home till 12 P.M. the business of the board having been kept back by the delay of the members in not meeting at the appointed hour.

Wednesday 8 Jan^y

At office meeting parties the Banker, Mr Ritchie etc — Preparing Estimate of Expenditure for this year — Attended Quarterly Meeting of Water Co^y — returned to office and went over the whole of Journal entries in last years a/cs — Examined detailed a/c for work done last year in Grounds buildings etc preparatory to making out discharge — Called on Mr Munro regarding various matters — Steamer arrived at 9 P.M. — and was rejoiced to learn that the dignity of a Baronet had been conferred on Mr Matheson.

Thursday 9 Jan^y

At office going over Dft Memorial regarding State of the Country with Mr Munro — was called upon by the Banker & Mr J McLeod regarding arrangements for a general illumination this evening & a public meeting in the Mason Hall in honour of Mr Matheson being created a Baronet — Wrote Rev^d Mr McRae with Dft of Memorial & Mr Mathesons letter on the subject — Went to Castle & arranged with Mrs Watson to have the building illuminated — Arranged various matters with Mr Howitt, gave books & maps to teachers. Went to Square and examined feet of ponies, was glad to see that they were much better & on a fair way to recovery William having given them more exercise of late outside — Returned to office and had meeting with McNab regarding his a/c for the Castle Works, wrote Mr D

Mackenzie Holm for an account of all cash materials etc given to McNab by Mr Scobie — also to Mr Gair for a/c of Steamer freights — Mr McNabs a/c for the Castle building amounts to £20,368.3/2 which with materials furnished such as Stone, Iron beams, Hardware etc, will amount to at least £30,000 — Attended meeting in the Mason Hall which was most respectable, and all seemed to rejoice in the honour paid to the Proprietor, this appeared even more evidently in the manner in which the illumination was conducted, every house was lighted even the most humble in Bayhead & Inaclate — There was not a window dark in Stornoway except Mr John Reid M^ckenzie's who is always an exception of every general rule however proper it may be —

Friday 10 Jan^y

Had meeting with Rev^d Mr McRae regarding draft of Memorial prepared by him & with Mr Munro's advise made several alterations on it — Attended meeting of Parochial Board at which the Dft Memorial was read over & approved of, the Free Church party not having appeared there was no opposition — arranged various other matters connected with the Board — Returned to the office to write letters, look over McNabs a/cs etc. etc.

Saturday 11 Jan^y

At office going over details of McNabs a/c for Castle as made up by Mr Binnie. The whole amount is for Castle

The whole amount is for Castle	£20368. 3. 2
Landing place Lodge	534. 5.10
Bathing House	38. 3. 7
	£20940.12. 7
of which he has received	£16011. 0 7
Leaving a balance due of	£4929.12 -

These a/cs are made up according to a scale of rates agreed upon by Mr Scobie & McNab and the quantities ascertained by Mr Binnies measurement. I cannot find out what has become of the first plans & Specification on which Mr McNab gave in his original offer — Examined Mr D Mackenzie — Alex Gair & McNab on the subject, but all of them say they saw them and had them in their possession but they cannot be found — Mr McKenzie says Mr Gair got them, Mr Gair that Mr McNab had them — Mr McNab that Mr Wilson got them — My reason in being so anxious to get the Specification is that they all say the proprietor by that Specification was bound to supply rubble Stones to the Contractor at a landing place near the site of building, also to supply nails for the Carpenter Work, neither of which stipulations appear in the new agreement with McNab — I have over & over again applied to Mr Scobie & Mr Wilson for the original Specification but to no effect. Mr Scobie however states that McNab was to be provided with Stones — It is clear the Specification can be traced to McNab & the fact of its disappearance and that he had something to do with it is rather suspicious. If McNab was bound to supply himself with Stones he would have now little or nothing to get, as the quarrying & carriage of the Stones have all along been paid by the proprietor — Went over the whole of contra a/cs with McNab for Materials, Steamer freights, Cash pay^{ts} etc. Attended meeting at Industrial School to view articles lodged there in order to be forwarded to Mr McDougall Inverness for the great exibition of 1851 — There are 24 articles lodged such as cloths manufactured in the Island, Stockings Shawls etc — I fear none of these articles are remarkable & worth sending to the exibition — Went over Memorial to Gov^t on State of Country & wrote the Rev^d Mr McRae Barvas & Mr Reid Lochs asking them to sign it in name of their boards — since writing the above saw (13 Jan^y) draft of original Specification which states that the Proprietor is to quarry stones & land them at the Cuddy point for the Contractor.

Monday 13 Jan^y

At office preparing estimate for working farms of Holm, Sand^k Hill for next crop also home farm & land now improving to be added to it — Having so much new land to lay down increases the expenditure very much, and not a corrisponding increase in the receipts. Going over rentals of land in the neighbourhood of Stornoway — Had meetings with various parties viz the Banker Mr Rod^k Nicolson, & Mr J M McLeod the latter about articles to be sent to Inverness to the exibition & price asked of property purchased from Collector McKenzie etc — Had meeting with Mr McNab who examined and certified his Cash a/c also account for Materials — Settled with him for various jobbing accounts, building additions to Captⁿ Burnabys Cottage, & materials furnished for various works for which I got a Stamp discharge from him so that nothing now remains unsettled except the Castle Works etc measured by Mr Binnie — was the remaining part of the evening writing letters for Steamer —

Tuesday 14 Jan^y

Preparing dispatches for Steamer till 12 noon — Arranging various matters as [sic] office & writing letters — Attended meetings of Gas Co^y, gas consumed last month amounted to £42, but all the disposable funds are still required for paying off the debt — Returned to office & was occupied meeting Rev^d Mr Reid Lochs on Poor Law business, Mr McLeod Valtos on various matters, Alexander Aignes who was so drunk that he did not know what he was saying or doing — going over last years a/cs & examining same —

Wednesday 15 Jan^y

Called on Mr Munro with George McLeod about taking up Poachers, Mr M's excuse for not going with these cases is the want of proper officers, he expects one by next Steamer. Consulted him on various subjects etc — Went to office and had consultation with Howitt regarding McNabs a/cs, ordered him to pay off all the men that could possibly be spared, and arranged regarding various matters — Had meetings with various parties Mr P Clark, Mr Ritchie, Contractors for Uig Road etc — Went over Rental of Stornoway Parish & examined same before being charged — Packet arrived received several letters, and answered same the mail being made up tonight —

Thursday 16th Jan^y

Went to patent Slip to see what foreman is about — Went to office & was engaged writing letters, Packet not having sailed — Had meeting with Mr John MacKenzie who offered to purchase the house & property now occupied by him at £420, being what was paid for it, also he offers £80 for the frontage to Cromwell Street of the Market stance say 50 feet back allowing the rest of the ground to remain as a market place with passage thereto but if at any time sold that he should have the first offer of it — The house property offered for, if not immediately sold require considerable repairs to be habitable — Mr James R McIver when in partnership with McLauchlan offered to feu the frontage of the market place at £7.10/- per annum to build a shop thereon, but McLauchlan having failed and involved Mr McIver in a heavy loss, besides other losses made by the herring fishing, the proposed building was not gone on with, but Mr McIver may be called upon for the feu duty of the past year — I asked Mr McKenzie to give in a written offer which he did & which will be forwarded to Sir James for his approval. Accompanied Mr John McLeod to Goat Hill to see ground occupied there by Mrs Wm Morison of which her lease expires at Whitsunday next, & of which she wishes a renewal — By the present lease certain improvements were to be made in the way of draining, and fences built for which the tenant was to be paid meliorations, the draining is said to have been done, but so ill executed that there is no improvement in the soil — The fences have been so ill built out of line & are in such bad repair that no meliorations can be due — The extent of the land is ten acres, the former rent £8.1/-, if a new lease be given I would propose the rent to be increased to £10 and the land to be properly improved by the tenant, the proprietor might perhaps give tiles, the tenant doing all the labour — 20/- per acre is a high rent in the present state of the ground one third being deep moss & quite soft & wet — Went to Rope Work Park to see ploughing & work doing there by Bowie. Walked over ground at Guirshader being drained & fenced by Houston & Co^y — Called at Mill which is quite full of grain — the Miller estimate[s] the grain crop of this year to be one third more than last which is so far pleasing — Went to meadow behind Castle to see draining doing there & now nearly Completed — Called at the Castle and went over the building with Mrs Watson, was sorry to observe almost in every room signs of damp and large quantities of water pooring [*sic*] in at the windows above & below in all the front rooms, must write Wilson as to this before settling with McNab — Went to Stables & was glad to see that the Gray ponies feet were almost well, arranged several matters with W^m McKay & Bowie etc. Returned to the office —

Friday 17th Jan^y

Went to office and wrote several letters for the Packet to Sir James Matheson, Mr Wilson Glasgow etc Had meetings with various parties about settlement of a/cs etc — Went to Soval to attend Poor Law Meeting — Mr Allan Ross was appointed Inspector, the Rev^d Mr Reid & I voted for Mr Wm Ross the Stornoway inspector, but were outvoted by the other members who held that the Inspector should reside in the Parish — Mr A Ross is in the mean time appointed Interim Inspector, the state of the votes being referred to the Board of Supervision to confirm Mr A Ross's appointment — Mr Ross is the Free Church Teacher of Lochs, which I stated as an objection to his holding the office of Inspector, as he could not faithfully perform both duties, to which he answered that he intended giving up his school — Mr Ross is a very respectable person & I have no doubt will perform his duty of inspector faithfully & regularly. The Memorial to Gov^t on the State of the Country was read & approved of by the Meeting — Went over the former Inspectors a/cs & find him to be due £19 to the Board, but which will be reduced to a few pounds if he produces vouchers for several items not allowed in his a/cs — Considered several applications for relief & admitted a few. The people of this parish (except the district of Carloway) are on the whole very well off, having still a few potatoes and plenty of fish — The people of Carloway are very poor & much crouded, a number of them should be sent to America — got home at 11 P.M.

Saturday 18th

Went to the office and was engaged going over rentals, writing letters, Called on Mr Munro regarding Shedden to consult him about sequestrating his Stock, he having never returned from the South & hearing that there are several parties here who have large claims against him, but resolved to delay taking Steps till the return of the Steamer in case he may come by her — Settling Steamer freights with Houston — Engaged the rest of the day with Mr D. MacKenzie. Meeting Christie regarding his a/cs, there is a balance of £152 due him by Mr D Mackenzie's shewing, but he has granted orders to various parties for a few pounds more than that amount, so that none of the money will go into his pocket — as he refused to grant a discharge in full I could not give him a settlement — He claims damages for the amount of work which he contracted for not having been gone on with, after he had provided part of the materials, but I think we convinced him that he had no claim & I think he would wave any demand on this ground, if met by a small sum of money to cover his loss in other respects — He says he has lost time in waiting a Settlement for more than two years — That Alexander Aignes prosicuted him for a debt, and recovered Interest damages & expences amounting to £40 which could have been prevented had he got a Settlement for the work done on the Estate, which Mr D Mackenzie answers by saying that it was Alex^r Gairs fault, that the delay was caused by his not measuring the work and making up his accounts, also that Christies money was arrested & nothing could be done till such was removed — Tho' I think Christie has no claim for the bridges not being gone on with, still I think his case deserves some consideration — I pressed him for a discharge & advised him against going to law, which he said he would not do, but would consider the matter for a few days. He offered to refer the matter to arbitration which I refused saying there was nothing to refer —

Monday 20 Jany 1851

Went to office and was engaged going over last years a/cs for Making & Repairing Roads, Repairs of House property in Stornoway etc — Went to Sappers office to examine plans of Reef & Kneep — Was remaining part of day going over Rental of Barvas Parish & Prepairing Estimate of Expenditure of this year — Reading Mr Gordons report on Education in Lews & making notes on Same — Arranging various matters with G McLeod G. officer, about statute labour, rent Collections, Bull money etc — Received three offers for Castle Terrace viz. J Christie & H Souter for £518.6.8. John Shaw & John McAulay for £1034. 18/4 and John McRae for £582.10/- & George McKenzie £1077.16/8.

Tuesday 21 Jan^y

Went to office and was engaged writing letters to Gerrie, McMillan, McDonald Ness, etc Gair etc. Meeting various parties vizt Howitt, Mrs Cameron regarding her son — Mrs Lees regarding her House — Mr Alex^r Morison regarding Free Church Charter — Mr Nov. McIver about Charter for Mrs Johnstons Ho — purchased from parties in Glasgow by his father — going over Rental accounts & preparing Estimate of next years Expences — wrote instructions for G McLeod G. Officer as to what works the Statute labour was to be applied in this Parish, & to Forbes foreman as to Statute labour in Uye district.

Wednesday 22 Jan^y

Went to office and was engaged settling a/cs with various parties — Going over Steamers a/cs with Mr Gair — The Steamers earnings at present can hardly meet the working expences, there being few passengers at this season of the year, and the goods traffic has greatly decreased, partly owing to the poor state of the Country & Highlands generally (the imports being now less than in former years), & partly by the effects of opposition, the greater part of the Goods & Passengers to Oban & Mull being conveyed by Steamers passing thro' the Crenan Canal — The Proprietor gets little or nothing now by the Steamer which in former times was a considerable portion of the Cargo — Wrote a second letter to various parties in arrear of freights to pay up immediately — Gave form of a/c to be made up by Mr Gair shewing receipts & Expenditure in each month since Steamer commenced in 1846 — Went with Mr Alex^r Morison to Mr Munros office and remained there for several hours revising draft of Free Church Charter for Manse & School Ground — which was signed by both parties & given to Mr Munro to forward to Edin^h to be extended — Consulted Mr Munro as to Christies a/cs, he confirms Christies statement that he paid £40 to Alexander for interest & expences on account of not being able to pay his debt — Returned to office & was engaged writing various parties   Rev^d Mr Hutchinson, Howitt etc etc — arranged with Rod^k Adam to build brickwork of Kiln at Braescalate Mill for 70/- — Reading papers regarding Harris Marches, etc.

Thursday 23 Jan^y

At office settling with country people for rents, kelp, etc — Writing various parties vizt J McDonald G.O. Uig regarding people at Deanston — Mr Cameron regarding Statute labour in Parish of Lochs — Mr Allan Ross regarding Hogarths poors rates — Wrote circulars to Ladies of Female Education Society to meet on Saturday — Meeting various parties Mr Munro about Road Money, arranged that Mr Rod^k Mackenzie shall make up the assessment list & collect the same — Rev^d Mr McRae Ness regarding deaf & dumb children sent by him from his Parish to Institutions in Edin^h and on State of the Country — Arranged with Howitt regarding various matters, safe to be built in office etc   Steamer arrived at 1/2 past 2 received letters from Sir James Matheson etc   Wrote to the Lochs, Uig and Barvas Ground officers at considerable length on emigration, stating the offer made to the people by the Proprietor and directing them immediately to make a tour of their several districts to ascertain what number will be got to emigrate volun[t]arily — There are two classes I would propose to emigrate, first all bad payers, say those two years in arrear of rent if able bodied & have no reasonable grounds of excuse for being so far in arrear — Secondly — I would propose to clear whole townships which are generally in arrear and are not conveniently situated for fishing and can be converted into grazings several of which are in the Parish of Uig — The difficulty in sending off the people next Spring who is to purchase their cattle, no dealer can be got to take them so early of the Season, they will be in such low condition that they cannot be driven to market — I fear the proprietor must take them and pay a proportion of their value the rest to go to meet arrears of rent —

Friday 24 Jan[y]

Went to Stoneyfield accompanied by Mr Ritchie, there is nothing doing on Sheddens farm, he has never returned since he went south in Dec[r] and I fear will never return, he has left his men unpaid and a/cs to a large amount with several of the Stornoway Shop Keepers, in fact he paid little or nothing of what he got, his stock & what little is due on his Contracts will I hope pay the years rent due — Went to Holm and walked over each field fixing the crop for next Season — Some of the fields are very wet & require still some draining Proceeded to the Tussoc grass, that transplanted last Season seems to be doing very well — The old grass is now being cut & used in feeding the Stock at Holm and is much relished — Walked over the different fields of Sandwick Hill & arranged for next years crop, Scotts sheep are there at present eating off the turnip — The young grass looks exceedingly well — Went to Bayhead and walked over ground there preparing for cropping, there is much work on it clearing off stones, levelling etc — Went to Square & inspected Workshops, Byres, Stables etc, pointed out to Mr Ritchie line of Carriage drive to be made by widening walk along outside of gardin to shorten distance to Landing place — Went to Castle & inspected hardware sent by Mr. Nisbit etc — arranged various matters with Mr Howitt — Went to office and had meeting with Mr Alex Morison Ropemaker who came with a deputation of the Bayhead people to ask for a Site for a school at or near Laxdale Bridge for the accommodation of the new Settlers — He says if two or three acres of land be given to the School Master, the Free Church will place one there, and that the children should be employed two hours each day cultivating and improving the teachers plot of ground with himself at their head, and thus teach the children habits of industry & an improved system of tillage — The Situation is a good one and every encouragement should be given to the people who have removed in order to induce the rest to follow their example, if the school succeeds & I have no fear but it will as Mr Morison says he & his party will take a deep interest in it a good example may be set to the rest of the country & on that account I would advise that a 19 year lease of two or three acres should be granted for such a purpose. I explained to Mr Morison what the Proprietor proposed doing in regard to emigration which he thinks well of[f] & says is a most liberal offer. I have no doubt but we will have his support — He recommends the Rev[d] Mr M[c]Lean late of Back as a fit person to be sent with the emigrants but recommends that the clergyman should not appear in the matter till all has been arranged as if he does he may not be acceptable to the People, emigration being as yet an unpopular subject, but that there should be a private arrangement with Mr McLean — In which opinion I think he is right — Was engaged meeting various Country people regarding Christies a/c — Had an interview with the Rev^d Mr McRae, conveyed Sir James message of thanks to him for his able assistance in drawing up Memorial to Gov^t, told him what the Proprietor proposed doing, he concurred at once in the opinion that it was folly to colonize together the people to be sent etc — Was complaining of the unsufficiency of the late repairs done to the Manse, that Mr McLeod Kingsborough was using them (the Presbytery) very badly and that he was sure there was some influence used etc — I denied the charge, that such could not be — He wished me to write to press Mr McLeod to give his award to which I replied that perhaps the [a]ward when given might not be satisfactory to him & remarked that perhaps he & I might agree to a proposal or compromise to be in the first place laid before Sir James for his approval & then given to Mr McLeod as what both parties would be satisfied with & he to pronounce accordingly — I proposed the Cottage with the addition of offices & land opposite which the Minister said would suit very well, but he would have preferred it before the Free Church School was built — I made no mention of a money allowance, but we fixed on Monday forenoon to meet to arrange a proposal — The whole was his own seeking & he brought on the subject — The Packet arrived received various letters & papers etc.

Saturday 25 Jan^y

Called on Mr Munro to consult him regarding my conversation with the Rev^d Mr McRae and as to future proceedings — He recommends that all proposals should come from Mr McRae and that in writing in the shape of a letter — Consulted Mr Munro regarding serving all whom we wished to emigrate with notices of removal which he thinks the safest course — Consulted him on various other matters Road Money, Rogue Money, letters regarding Harris Marches from Mr Cheyne etc — Went to office had meeting with Mr Gair on Steamer Matters — Went to Bank & negotiated credits — Attended meeting of ladies at Industrial School, the vaccancies in Lady Mathesons class were filled up — There is a great increased desire to attend to the Ayrshire Needle work, and tho' ten of the best hands have been employed at Lady Mathesons dress the sum of £2.12/- was earned last month at other work — The school seems well attended — Had conversations with several parties about Emigration and all declared Sir James proposal to be a most liberal one & calculated for the peoples good — Returned to the office and was engaged meeting several parties, and writing letters for the Packet etc — Gave instructions to G McLeod to make a round of the Parish to ascertain the number willing to emigrate & gave him a list Showing the arrears & told him to intimate to all in arrear two years rent that they must prepare to leave the Country.

Monday 27 Jan^y

Went to Steamer & Steamer office to arrange some business with Mr Gair — Went to office and had meeting with Mr Munro regarding Road Money, Mr. Cheynes letters, etc — with the Rev^d Mr McRae regarding the Glebe case when we arranged (subject to the approval of the Proprietor & Presbytery) that on Captn Burnabys leaving the Island he should remove to the Cottage and get 8 Scotch Acres of land adjoining to it, that opposite the cottage & between the Bayhead New Road & Bayhead feus, in exchange for the Manse & Glebe of Tong with an annual payment of £38 as compensation for Grass glebe, being the average of £49.10/- and £26.10/-, the respective valuations on which the arbiters differed. The Cottage to be put into a good state of repair & the present Stable to be added to the house — offices on a small scale to be built for the Minister and the whole ground to be well enclosed with a Stone fence — Had a call from Captn Burnaby, Mr J. R. MacIver, Mr Munro — went to Ordinance [sic] office to examine plans regarding Harris March to get names & information for Mr Cheyne — Sent for John McKay to get proper spelling & meaning of names — remained at office till 6 P.M. [sic] next morning preparing dispatches for Steamer having the letters of three mails & Steamer letters to answer —

Tuesday 28 Jan^y

Went to office and got ready dispatches for Steamer which sailed at 1/2 past 12 — At Steamer office arranging disputes regarding missing egg boxes — Had conversation with the Rev^d Mr Campbell Uig on the State of the Country — and explained to him what the proprietor proposed doing in regard to emigration, with which he seemed satisfied and said that a number in his parish were rather disposed to Emigrate, which he saw the wisest plan for many of them — Had meeting with Captn McKenzie regarding Stornoway House property, he being on the look out for a house to buy. He says he has not given up hopes of getting Holm — Saw Brock who called with his journal of what he has been doing — arranged form for him to Shew number of vermin killed, game, etc. Had meeting with Scaliscro and arranged with him terms of Lease for Reef, Island of Floda and Ardmore, to meet again tomorrow to arrange finally — Mr Munro having gone by the Steamer arranged with Mr Ross about sequestrating Sheddens effects at Stone[y]field, other parties are now proceeding against him and if I do not sequestrate in name of the Proprietor I may lose recourse Arranged rate of assessment for Road Money — Had meeting with several parties on various subjects —

Wednesday 29

Went to office and had meeting with Howitt & Alex^r Mackenzie regarding work done by the latter at Soval & Aline Stables & Coach House, he not having finished them according to Contract I delayed a settlement till the same was completed — Sent Howitt to inspect the work with him, with the view of making a final settlement with the Contractor — Spent the greater part of the day arranging with McRae Scaliscro for lease of Reef & Ardmore, there is a difference of £5 between us — he wants the rent of the Island of Floda to be included in the rent of £120, but I stand out for an additional rent for the Island   Arranged all but this, separated without coming to an agreement — Had meeting with Alexander about his farm, and gave him a letter allowing him ten days to make up his mind and if he did not agree to the terms offered him by that time his farm would be advertised to let — Warned him that he would be held liable in damages if he turned up more land than if he was to continue tenant of the farm next year — Writing letters to various parties — Going over Estimate of expenditure for next year for Working farms in proprietors hands, Land improvements etc. Called on Mr Ross regarding sequestration of Sheddens effects —

Thursday 30 Jan^y

Went to office & had meeting with Mr J M McLeod regarding land occupied by Mrs Wm Morison of which she wants a new lease, but defer giving an answer till I hear from Sir J Matheson — Had another lengthened interview with Scaliscro but parted as we met there being still a difference of £5 between us — Had a meeting with McRae Melista regarding payment of the meliorations payable under his old lease — With Mr Gerrie regarding Tolsta & Uig Roads — with Rev^d Mr Murray Uye who called to pay his feu duty — explained to him what Sir James proposed regarding emigration & which he seemed to think well of — etc — Going over rental accounts, Meal and Seed a/cs — Writing letters etc — Called on Mr Ross to look after McLauchlan for shop rent & Steamer freights as I hear he is to leave by next Steamer & having written him twice without an answer — Reading over Memorial regarding Harris Marches —

Friday 31 Jan^y

Had meeting with Christopher McRae Mealista who with his brother were formerly sub tenants of Mr McRae Huishinish who prior to Whit^y, 1849 held the lease of Mealista, the meliorations (£45) are payable to him, therefore told Christopher that he must get a letter from Mr McRae authorising him to receive & grant a receipt for the meliorations before they can be paid to him — Had meeting with McRae Scaliscro who at last agreed to the rent asked by me, and I accepted his offer with the addition of £5 for the Island of Flodda subject to the approval of Sir James Matheson the total yearly rent being £125 — The tenant to get meliorations at the end of his lease for building House, Fanks, etc to the extent of £150 if then found to be worth so much — a march dyke to be built for him between Reef & Kneep — His stock to be taken at valuation on the termination of his lease but not at the break in the end of the seventh year — Went over & minutely examined the Estimate for next year of expenditure for Grounds, Plantations, Farms in Proprietors hands & drainage works & made reductions where practicable — Examined a/cs of expenditure for last month and granted orders for payment of same — Had meeting with Rod^k MacKenzie regarding Road Money, went over valuation of property & assessment with Alex McKenzie & James Anderson Valuators and arranged same. Packet arrived — received letters from Sir James —

enumeration districts, giving
—undaries of each Name of
—erator, with probable Numbe—
—nes & inhabitants —

Friday 16 Dec. 14

the people of Aonlista, and Mig—
—adu Gaeshadu Inaclute,
—adu, and having explained
—nditions on which they were
—emigrated, their Conditions
—s of Arrears in the following
—its were arrived at —

	No of families to be removed	Arrears	Souls	Value
—sta	6	£ 34.8.4	44	£ 16.
—s	8	41.10.10	43	68.
—du	2	22.1.6	11	3.
—du	2	19.15.7	4	10.
—ute	1	1.10	8	—

— the Manse at 7 P.M. walked to
— and took boat for Barvera,
—nculute at 10 P.M. blowing a

Saturday 1 Feb^y

Went to Keith Street to see about a feu for Mrs John McRae removing from
Bayhead — Called to Mrs Mathesons School — Had a meeting with Mr
John Mackenzie & told him that Sir James had accepted his offer for the
House he now occupied but not for the front of the Market place the price
offered being so small — To which he replied that he could not think of
taking the one without the other and that it was with the view of getting the
feu purchased from Miss Chrichton that he offered so much for the other
property — He then offered the price paid for the Market feu if he got the
whole land, and to pay in addition the value of the stalls or sheds built behind
and to keep them open to the public so long as they would let — Considering
that the other property requires such extensive repairs, that it is desirable to
get quit of such old house property and that he now offers the full price paid
for the Market Stance I would recommend to let him have it — a Market
Place might be made opposite the Counting House there is space enough and
a better situation — Had a meeting with Mr John McAulay who declined
giving a greater rent than £15 for the ground near the Episcopal Chapel, after
a long argument on both sides agreed to let him have the next crop at the rent
offered, as it is now far in the Season and as he pays the rent from Martinmas
last — Had meeting with Alexander regarding settlement of his a/c during
Mr Scobies management and wrote Mr D MacKenzie on the subject —
Preparing Estimate of Expenditure for this year, going over last years a/cs—
Writing letters etc — Had meeting with parties wishing to farm land behind
Inaclate.

Monday 3 Feb^y

Had a meeting with a Club of respectable tradesmen who wish to farm the
land East of Sand^k Road, about 20 acres between John McAulays land & my
farm Walked over the ground with them, a considerable portion of it has
been trenched this year & was never cropped, I told them they would get it
at 30/- per acre & be bound to farm it in a proper manner — They offered
20/- per acre & to get a 15 year lease which I declined — To a farmer & in
any other situation the rent they offer is enough, considering that the greater
part of the land is deep moss & what is hard is new land and requires an extra
quantity of manure for several years to come, but tradesmen having small
plots should pay at a higher rate than one who must make his living by land
— Went to office and had a call from the Rev^d Mr Hutchinson who went over
his usual complaints which amount to little or nothing — Meeting Mr Howitt
Mr Cameron Mr Nicolson etc — went to Guirshader & Ropework Park to
see ploughing & clearing of Stones doing by Bowie — Inspected trenching
& draining going on at these places, visited several of the new Houses built
by the Bayhead people who seem pleased with the change they have made
— Inspected Houses building for Widows — Went over and made list of

those still to remove & for whom houses must be procured   Went to Castle and inspected work now doing by painters — arranged various matters with Mr Howitt — Went to Stables and inspected same, the Gray ponys feet are all but well — Went over Work Shops & offices pointed out several small things to be done — Went to office and examined the Collectors & Inspectors Books of Uig Parochial Board, the receipts for last year are £150.6/9 the Amount of Expenditure £184.6/-. And the arrears of assessment £103.8/0 — It is to be feared the Expenditure of this year will be more — Wrote letters to various parties — Going over and Examining last years account —

Tuesday 4 Feb^y

At office writing letters — Meeting with Howitt, Fairbairn & various Contractors   Attended Meeting of Poor Law Board — there being none but Anti Emigrationists present they wished to disapprove of the Memorial & what had been done at the former meeting, which motion I opposed on the ground that they should have attended the meeting and then & there objected, that what had been done could not now be undone & that they should not say anything against the Memorial till they had seen it — The Inspector was then ordered to engross the Memorial & further discussion of this subject was delayed till next meeting to be held this day month — Returned to office and had meeting with Alex^r M^ckenzie regarding a Settlement of his a/c — With Fairbairn & Munro the Miller regarding their Meal a/cs — Preparing Estimate of this years Expenditure which is delayed by being so much interupted by other business — Completed examination of last years accounts —

Wednesday 5 Feb^y

Went to office and was engaged at Estimate for this years expenditure — Had meeting with various parties Mr Nicolson, the Sheriff, Mr R. Mackenzie & Mr J Gair — Was engaged the remaining part of the day at Mr Scobies a/cs with Mr D Mackenzie, had a lengthened interview with Mr J R McIver but did not come to a settlement there being questions as to the price of meal & salt to be referred to Mr Scobie — Settled with Alexander a balance of £103 for work done & farm produce supplied during Mr Scobie's management — Had meeting with Alexander Gair who is still here waiting a settlement of his a/c — Mr D Mackenzie says he should not be paid till his accounts for wood, lime, etc are examined in case he may not be able to account for all, but I suspect he wishes to keep Gair here thinking that he will be paid to the date of Settlement — I have given him nothing to do for the last 12 months — I do think some understanding should be come to with Mr Scobie as to who is to be liable for Mr D Mackenzie's salary and the people employed under him, as there seems to be no prospect of their bringing matters to a close & I cannot understand how they employ their time — There are still many a/cs to settle with parties here which I have not & cannot get out of D. Mackenzies hands — I wrote to Mr Callender on this subject some time ago but have not had his reply — Mr D Mackenzie seemed rather exighted today & had evidently been "tasting" in the forenoon (Leave this out in Mr M's copy) Packet arrived, received letters from Sir James —

Thursday 6 Feb^y

Went to office and was engaged settling with people from Bayble and Shader for work done on their crofts — Settled with Mrs Aulay MacAulay about removing her house at Bayhead — Had meeting with Rev^d Mr Campbell of Uig & conversed with him on State of the Country, Dr Beggs letter of which he does not approve — He seems favourable to emigration & thinks a number will go from his parish — Had meeting with Alex^r Mackenzie regarding a Settlement of his a/c for Soval & Aline Coach House, this business should have been arranged long ere now, but the money was arrested in my hands & McKenzie knowing that he was not to handle the cash was in no hurry to complete the work, which I have now got done at his expence — He has a balance to get of about £18 — Wrote Alexander declining his offer for Aignish Farm vizt £100 & to build a new Steading etc — said the proprietor might accept that rent provided he was content with the present Steading & made any outlay necessary himself — Meeting various parties — Going over and examining Meal, Cattle & Store a/cs for last year — Had meeting with Mr Gair about Steamer freights, with Mr Ross about shutting up Roads at Ba[y]head and Guirshader, Steamer arrived at 1/2 past 3 — Was engaged at office till 11 P.M. Writing letters for Packet to Mr Souter etc.

Friday 7 Feb^y

Went to Holm to arrange with Mr D Mackenzie about filling up Schedule for Sir John McNeill and explained to him how it was to be done — Went over Farm with McIntosh the cattle fed on the Tussoc grass are thriving very well — This farm is still very wet and a great part requires to be redrained — Had a meeting with Sheddens son & Farm servant who came to ask for provender for their Horses — I told them that if they sent the Horses to the Castle Farm they would get food for their work as what they had already got had not been paid for — Called on the Sheriff to consult him on various subjects — Went to office & met Howitt, G McLeod, Humphrey, Rev^d Mr Hutchinson to settle for meal got by him — Rev^d Mr Campbell Uig — Arranged with McRae Arinish & got him to sign a letter agreeing to accept of £5 per annum as Compensation for ground to be taken by Commissioners of N. Lights, they now restrict the quantity of ground to the mere site of the Houses with a Road leading from them to the landing place; in that case the Proprietor may lower the feu duty to one half say £6 — Wrote Mr J Reid M^ckenzie denying my liability as Baron Baillie to repair his pier, and called on him to put that erection in a safe state for the safety of the lieges — Had meeting with Alexander about his Farm, allowed him till Monday first to think of it — going over various a/cs —

Saturday 8 Feb^y

Went to office and was engaged going over accounts and rentals with the view of preparing Schedule for Sir John McNeill — Had meeting with the Banker, Mr Wm Ross etc — Preparing notices for Shutting up Roads at Bayhead — The remaining part of the day completing Estimate of expenditure for this year — and going over Cash book for last month —

Sunday 9 Feb^y

Broke came to tell me that "Bella" the pet deer had been missing yesterday and that he thought she had strayed till this morning when her head & intestings were discovered in a drain behind the Laundry and the two fore quarters hid in the valley between the new Bridge & the Ice Hous[e], the hind quarters having been removed and neatly and well skinned, the person who had done the rascally act seemingly was in no hurry but went very cooly to work — In the enclosure where the deer was kept is found a large stone, pointed at one end covered with blood — There is a mark on the forehead of the deer shewing evidently that she was killed with this stone — foot marks are found in the enclosure, which I told Broke to be well observed, also to leave the remains of the deer where it had been hid in the wood, and to keep watch tonight in case the thief might come back for the fore quarters. Called on Mr Ross (Mr Munro being from home) to set his office on the outlook — This is one of the greatest outrages I have heard of being comitted here — and it is to be hoped the perpetrator will be discovered —

Monday 10 Feb^y

At office all day preparing schedule for Sir J McNeill which was completed so far as the accounts were in our possession. Completing estimate of expenditure for currant year — Meeting Mr Ross about deer — Instructed him to get warrants of search against all suspicious parties Sent Howitt to Soval there being some suspicion in that quarter — He examined the house minutely his excuse being that he wanted to see what painting & repairs it required, but found nothing & from Rod^{ks} conduct he thinks he is inosent — Engaged with Mr Gair at Steamer a/cs — Preparing dispatches for Steamer till 3 A.M.

Tuesday 11

Preparing Steamer dispatches till 12 when she sailed — Had meetings with various parties — and wrote Several letters — Started for Callanish at 2 P.M. When passing Deanston meet Mr Ross with two sheriff officers who had been searching John McLeod Majors house at Achmore & who had with them a Considerable quantity of fresh meat which they supposed to be venison, but when examined by Mr Cameron & I we at once saw it was mutton and fore quarters — The part taken away of the deer was hind quarters — McLeod when asked by the officers to account for how he got the fresh meat told them it was a deer he had killed on the hill, when asked for the Skin he replied that he was not in the habit of taking home the skin this was all said to blind the officers as it was evidently stollen mutton — I told Mr Ross tho' I was satisfied the flesh found in McLeod's house was no part of the deer, still he should not let the matter rest, as McLeod must account for how he came by the mutton — Proceeded to Callanish and attended a meeting of the Uig Parochial Board, and laid on an assessment for the current year at 1/6 per pound one half payable by the landlord & one half by the tenant — I was for making the assessment 2/- but the other members were for keeping it at the present rate, My fear is that the assessment laid on will not meet the demands —

Wednesday 12

Wrote letters to Stornoway, afterwards proceeded to Reef and saw Cattle now wintering there and looking very well — Walked over March proposed by Mr Cameron between Reef & Kneep but did not approve of it, tho' no doubt the most natural boundary, as it cut too much of the pasture land off the latter place. I think Kneep can be cleared, and the whole pasture attached to it may be added to Reef which will improve that farm very much — There are several in Kneep far behind in arrears of rent and some in Valtos, those should be sent to America, and those remaining in Kneep removed to Valtos in place [of] the emigrants from that place — The greater part of the arable land of Kneep being adjoining to that of Valtos to continue in the possession of the Small tenants — By this arrangement Valtos would be the only township of small tenants left in the peninsula of Fourteen Pence — Valtos is the best fishing port in Uig, and if small tenants can do in Uig, they should be able to support themselves here and pay their rents — Went to the Valtos School house, and with Mr. Cameron & the Ground officer's assistance went over the circumstances and condition of each family in Kneep and Valtos, examining the State of their arrears, stock, etc — Explained to them the conditions offered them if they emigrated, their desparate prospects if they remained here, and the good prospects before them in America etc etc — From Kneep the number of families which we fixed on to emigrate is six, only one consenting — the number of souls 43, the total of the 6 families arrears £74 and the probable value of their Stock £27.5/- All these are destitute except one family and have now little or no food — From Valtos we fixed on sending 8 families only one consenting, the number of souls 50 — Total of arrears £111.15/- and value of their stock £39.15/-. The greater number of these are also destitute — They are also very ill off for Clothing and the value of their Stock will no purchase enou[g]h for them — Got to the Free Church Manse at 9 P.M. and remained there for the night — Mr & Mrs Campbell are absent in Stornoway

Thursday 13 Feb[y]

Walked to the Manse of Uig and found Mr Watson busy planting potatoes, and clearing his arable land of Stones with a number of men employed. Went to the Parish School & found it quite crouded there being more than 40 schollars present, and on enquiring the cause was told that Mr Watson gave notice to the people that unless they sent their children to school he would pindfold every sheep & cow of theirs he found on his grass — He expects to get the parents to attend his Church in the same way but I fear he will be disappointed — Met with the people of Braenish, Islivick, Mangersta & Carnish and explained to them the condition on which they were to emigrate — Went over and examined the condition & circumstances of each family, the amount of their arrears, value of Stock etc, and arrived at the following results — We fixed on sending four families from Braenish none consenting, the number of souls 27 — The total of their arrears £52-0-10 — and the value of their Stock £6-5/- — From Islivick 3 families are to be removed consisting of 18 souls none consenting — The total of their arrears is £54-9-4 and the value of their stock £14-5/-. From Mangersta we fixed on sending six families composed of 34 souls two consenting, the total of their arrears £72-15/5 and the probable value of their Stock £38-12/- — From Carnish we fixed on sending 12 families (five consenting) consisting of 61 souls The total of their arrears £183-10/8 and the probable value of their Stock £57-5/-. The greater part of the people fixed on today for America are even now destitute of food, several families have not even one meal of food — Carnish should be cleared altogether, the people left can be sent to Mangersta & Islivick in place of those to be removed, Carnish would make a good addition to Ederoel adjoining — received a dispatch from the Sheriff with a parcel containing the Census pa[s]pers — With Mr Camerons assistance divided the whole island into enumeration districts, giving the boundaries of each & name of enumerator, with probable number of houses & inhabitants —

Friday 14 Feb[y]

Met the people of Croulista, Aird Uig, Carishader, Gaeshader, Enaclate, Ungishader and having explained the conditions on which they were to be emigrated, their condition state of arrears etc the following results were arrived at —

	No of families to be removed	Arrears	Souls	Value of Stock	Willing
Crousista [sic]	6	£34. 8. 4	44	£16.15	4
Aird Uig	8	41.10.10	43	68. 0	6
Carishader	2	22. 1. 6	11	3.10/-	2
Gaeshader	2	19.19. 7	4	10.10/-	1
Enaclate	1	1.10/-	8	—	1

Left the Manse at 7 P.M.   Walked to Keanlangavat and took boat for Barnera, arrived at Hacalete at 10 P.M.   Blowing a gale —

Saturday 15 Feb[y]

Met with all the people of Barnera composing the Townships of Bosta, Tobson, Ballagloum, Braeclate and Croir also the people of Crulivig & Earshader on the Main, and having addressed them explaining the conditions offered — examined as usual into the state & circumstances of each family arrived at the following results

	No of Families to Emigrate	Souls	Arrears	Value of Stock	Willing
Bosta	0	0	0	0	0
Tobson	8	59	£93. 3/-	£37.10/-	1
Ballagloum	4	31	15.17/8	31.10/-	1
Braeclate	6	35	62. 9/8	22. 5/-	1
Croir	0	0	0	0	0
Crulivig	2	15	13.16/ 6	12.15/-	2

Ballagloum & Braeclate can be cleared & those now remaining put into Tobson, these two small township[s] would make a good addition to Haclate, being adjoining & natural boundaries — Crulivig can be cleared & added to Linshader — Took boat for Callanish and got home at 10 P.M. The people of Uig upon the whole are not more in arrear of rent that [sic] the other parts of the Island — The quantity of meal which they got on C[r] in 1846- & 47, and still unpaid is what leaves them so much in debt — The greater number of them deny the quantity charged against them & many assert that they paid the meal when they got it to James & John M[c]kenzie Ederoel then ground officers — Neither John nor James can read or write and it was quite impossible they could keep account of the meal given out & from whom they got payment, I have great doubts as to all being right in that quarter — The remaining tenants of Aird Uig except one family followed me to Barnera to volunteer to emigrate, so that farm will be clear at Whitsunday — Those fixed on to Emigrate in this Parish are the most destitute, most in arrear of Rent and have least Stock — They cannot pay rents so that it is the wisest measure to send them off, as they are now a burdin to their neighbours, and they or their families may soon come on the Parish — They are all able to emigrate if willing — We in all cases avoided including in our lists families that could not emigrate if the heads were too old, or the children too young — The Steamer should be sent round to Loch Roag to take them on board, as it would save the emigrants much trouble & expence by going to Stornoway — and we could calculate on more going, as some might be dissuaded from proceeding by their friends or pretended friends in Storn[y] including the Stornoway merchants who are talking of getting warrants to stop those in their debt —

Monday 17

Went to the office and saw what had been done in my absence, arranged various matters — Held a Baron Baillie Court to hear appeals against payment of Road Money, there were only two which were refused — Returned to the office and was engaged meeting parties Mr Nicolson, the Banker, Howitt, Ritchie — The Rev[d] Mr M[c]Rae & accompanied him to the ground proposed to be given for a glebe which we walked over — There is a meeting of Presbytery called at Barvas this day week to arrange this matter — Went over various a/cs and granted orders for payment of same — Wrote letters for Packet — Left for Callanish at 7 P.M.

Tuesday 18

At Callanish met the tenants of that township, Garynahine, Deanston & Braescalate, and having given them all the necessary information about emigration and the terms offered by the proprietor, proceeded to examine[d] how each tenant stood and the value of the Stock of those in arrear — The people of Braescalate & Garynahine are very industrious & their rents well paid up — They have also plenty of room, as none volunteered in these two Townships I did not ask them to emigrate — The following is the result of our examination in the other two Townships, viz

	No of Families to Emigrate	Souls	Arrears	Value of Stock	Families willing
Callanish	6	33	£26. 4. 2.	£17.-.-.	5
Deanston	4 [*No figures shown*]		51.18. 7.	4.10.-	4

34

Those going from Deanston are some of the Reef men who removed there last year, after building new Houses they have volunteered to Emigrate — Proceeded to Dune Carloway and there met the people of Tolsta Cailish, Dune Carloway, Kerriwick, Knock Carloway, Upper Carloway, Borrowston & Garinnan and having as usual explained the nature of the Emigration measures to be carried out, and examined the state of each tenants account the following results were arrived at

	No of Families to Emigrate	Souls	Arrears	Value of Stock	Families willing
T. Cailish	7	39	£25.12. 9.	£22. 5. 0.	3
D. Carloway	8	49	37. 8. 10.	31.15.0	2
Kerriwick	2	13	12.10. 7.	19.-.-.	1
K. Carloway	7	41	52.12. 7.	62.15.-.	2
Up. Carloway	10	55	85. 8. 5.	54.-.-.	2
Borrowston	8	32	47.17. 1.	46.15.-.	—
Garinnan	2	11	6. 6.-.	15.10.-.	1

All these are fishing vill[i]ages except the first & last, and are more in arrear of rent, than those that do not fish, caused in my opinion by the people being neither fishers nor farmers, their time attention & support being divided between the two. The people in general seem much better as to food than in former years, and are not willing to confess that they will be short of food before next crop for fear of being sent to America — I invariably tell all who do not accept the offer now made them need not expect assistance of any kind either in foor [sic] or seed, and that they must wholly depend on their own resources which will be a good answer to make to beggers in future. Dune Carloway is a good grazing farm & may be cleared of those remaining by filling up the blanks in the other Townships — Got to Dalbeg at 11 P.M.

Wednesday 19

At Dalbeg met the people of Dalmore and having proceeded as usual fixed on 11 families to emigrate consisting of 53 souls amount of arrears £107.5.2 value of Stock £84.15.-. 4 Families are willing to emigrate —
Dalmore tho' much improved by the Dest. Com[ees] operations is a most unhealthy place, every mail [sic] head of a family having been twice married, and several have lost their second wives — There does not appear to be a healthy man in it except an old pensioner who served in Egypt — all seem consumptive — I advised them all to emigrate but found them very reluctant tho' they themselves told me of the above facts — They are also much in arrear of rent — This farm should be cleared & added to Dalbeg being a good sheep grasing & would add much to the value of Dalbeg which is now rather contracted in its boundaries — Proceeded to Shawbost school which I found quite crouded & attended by upwards of 100 children — Inspected the work

doing at Shawbost Quay which is proceeding rather slowly being all tide work — Had a meeting in the School House with the people of Arnold, North & South Bragar & South Shawbost and having addressed them as [*sic*] some length, examined the state of their accounts, how as to food etc etc fixed on the following numbers to emigrate

	No of families to Emigrate	Souls	Arrears	Value of Stock	Families willing to Emigrate
Arnold	6	34	£46. 6. 2.	£46. 5. 0.	—
N. Bragar	12	61	142. 8.10.	62. 5.-.	1
S. Bragar	11	63	68.13. 4.	45.10.-.	—
S. Shawbost	7	37	42.16. 3.	33. 5.-.	3

These townships are very popelous and would be difficult to clear, besides there would be no object gained as they are more suitable for Small tenants than anything else — If the above bad payer were removed, the rest I have no doubt can pay in ordinary times, but as they altogether depend on the price of Cattle to pay their rents they are hard pressed in those days — Returned to Dalbeg at 10 P.M. —

Thursday 20

Remained at Dalbeg during the forenoon making up our schedules etc Went to North Shawbost and met the people of that township, examined their accounts etc fixed with 6 families to emigrate, consisting of 32 souls, the amount of their arrears being £72.2.4. and the value of their stock £10.-.-. 6 families volunteered — Proceeded to Barvas & arrived at the Manse at 8 P.M.

Friday 21

At the Barvas School House met the people of Brue, Upper & Lower Barvas, Upper & Lower Shader, and having gone through the usual course fixed on the following numbers to emigrate from each place —

	No of Families to emigrate	Souls	Arrears	Value of Stock	Willing
Up. Barvas	[*No entries shown in diary*]				
Lower Barvas	13	79	£149.13. 3	£66. 5.0.	6
Up Shader	6	42	86.12. 8.	55.15.-.	—
Lower Shader	13	71	169. 6. 2	67. 5.-.	2

Received Steamer dispatches at Barvas & in consequens returned home at 1 A.M. — The above mentioned arrears in all the Townships is not only arrears of rent but is greatly increased by Meal given on C^r by Mr Scobie & seeds & potatoes given to the people both during his & my management.

Saturday 22

Went to office & had meeting with McLennan the old Shepherd at Kean Reasort who came to ask for a free passage to America, but which I thought proper to decline as I understand he has means of his own. Examined what has been doing in my absence, had meeting with Mr Munro regarding the Glebe Case, Sheddens affairs etc etc — With McLeod Valtos regarding matters in his Parish, Howitt regarding McNabs a/c etc etc — Going over lists of parties who are to get summonses of removal — Had meeting with Mr J Gair regarding Steamer a/cs —

Monday 24

Went to office and was engaged writing the Moderator of the Presbytery proposal regarding excambion of Glebe etc — Meeting various parties vizt Rev^d Mr Hutchinson, Howitt, Mr Munro etc Preparing dispatches for the Steamer till 2 A.M. — Went over last years a/cs which are now completed, & ready to send by Steamer tomorrow to Mr Callender —

Tuesday 25

At office writing letters for Steamer till 12 noon — Had meeting with Messrs McDonald & Thomson Buckie, regarding Holm Curing Houses, told them they would get them at a yearly rent of £24 or £12 to 1st June — They are to go to Holm to see the Houses & call again. Had meeting with Mr McAulay Linshader regarding interest charged him for Expenditure on works done during Mr Scobies management & which he says is overcharged — I wrote to Mr D Mackenzie on this subject — Attended a meeting of the Gas Co^y, the works seem to do little more than pay working expences — I fear they will never do well under the present management — Renewed Mrs Watts Bill — Walked over ground now being drained at Bayhead and Guirshader, over plantations between Mill & Keepers Lodge where some planting is now going on — Went to Castle & saw work doing by painters. Inspected Stables, bires, workshops etc — Returned to the office & met Rigg Coll — McDonald Fish Curer etc etc

Wednesday 26th

Went to the office and arranged various matters with Mr Ritchie, Mr Howitt and Mr Morison Proceeded to Barvas and attended a poor Law Meeting, intended to have held a meeting with the people of Borve, but not feeling well put off the meeting till tomorrow — Went on to Galson & arrived there at 10 P.M. accompanied by Captⁿ Burnaby & Mr Cameron —

Thursday 27

At the School House of Borve meet the people of Five Penny Borve, Mid Borve, Melbost Borve & North Galson, and having addressed them as usual proceeded to examine their a/cs and fixed on the following numbers from these places, vizt

	No of Families to Emigrate	Souls	Arrears	Value of Stock	Willing
F. Penny Borve	6	36	£72. 3. 4.	£21.15.0.	0
Mid Borve	3	18	35.18. 3.	33. 0.0.	0
Melbost Borve	9	37	74. 2. 9.	68.15.0.	2
N. Galson	6	24	38.19. 9.	31.10.0.	1

The people of F.P. Borve are much in arrear of rent but they have still a good stock of Sheep & Cattle — The people of Mid Borve are destitute of all means of support & also much in arrear of rent — The people of Melbost Borve are not quite so ill off, tho' much in arrear — The North Galson people are more industrious than those of Borve but very poor — Few are for emigrating tho' many of them will be quite destitute of food this season — Proceeded to Swanabost & met the people of Cross and Swanabost and having explained the terms & reasons for Emigration and examined their accounts fixed on the following

	No of Families to Emigrate	Souls	Arrears	Value of Stock	Families Willing
Swanabost	7	54	£80.10. 7.	£15.-.-.	6
Cross	2	15	17. 6.11.	11.10.-.	0

Those who wish to emigrate from Swanabost are people who removed from Uig nearly 20 years ago — They are now comparatively comfortable but are most anxious to Emigrate — Not so the Ness Men who are determined to a man not to leave the Country on any account — some of them are much in arrear of rent & if they do not emigrate must be deprived of their land if they do not pay up their arrears — fixed on 11 to be summoned out if they do not pay up —

Friday 28 Feb[y]

At Swanabost met the people of North and South Dell, Hawbost, Lionel, Eoropie, Five Penny Ness, KnockAird, — Having explained to them, the parties who were to be deprived of land, and the conditions on which they were to be sent to America, got few or none to agree to voluntary emigration — The greater number of the people of these places are fishermen, and can pay their rents if inclined. We fixed on the following to go to America who are not fishermen, vizt.

	No of Families to Emigrate	Souls	Arrears	Value of Stock	Families Willing
South Dell	—	—	—	—	—
North Dell	1	5	£10. 1. 2.	-. -. -.	0
Hawbost	2	10	18.19. 2	£31. 1. 0.	0
Lionel	1	10	8.13. 0.	9. 2. -.	0
Eoropie	3	11	29. 2. 4.	21. 5. -.	0
F.P. Ness	6	29	63. 5.11.	43.15. -.	0
KnockAird	0	0	-. -. -.	-. -. -.	0

Besides the above I fixed on depriving 79 fishermen of their lands if they do not pay up their arrears of rent, or get the Fish Curers to become bound for the payment of their rents — Many of the Ness men are supposed to have money in bank tho' in arrear of rent but they must pay up now or want land

...oned to Carlsbad in place of the
to America — Attended a meet[ing]
Gas & Water Coy — Went to Steamer
...e various matters with the Capt[ain]
...g despatches till 3 A.M. —

Tuesday 25 March

[Off]ice writing despatches for Steam[er]
...Noon — Went by Steamer to toil...
...landed at [Jenneray], and too[k]
to Stenneway where I met the Re...
...[Atkinson] at the Cottage, which
...bad state of repair, and seems
...been well finished — The floors
...rooms are very bad being very
...[Composed] of Clay & rock — Agree
...d both rooms & line one of the
...wood, put in fixed beds, & pu...
...small place at the end of the
...[place] for dogs, the whole work no
...ed £15 to £20 — This Cottage is ...

Saturday 1 March

Met the people of Callicvol, Skeggersta and Quishader and fixed on depriving the following numbers in each place of land and sending them to America but few or none agreed to go

	No of Families to Emigrate	Souls	Arrears	Value of Stock	Families Willing
Callicvol	1	3	£4. 3. 1.	£1.10. -.	1
Skeggersta	—	—	-. -. -.	-. -. -.	—
Quishader	—	—	-. -. -.	-. -. -.	—

Besides these I fixed on depriving 12 people of their lands for non payment of rents the greater number of them being fishermen there is no excuse for their being in arrear of rent, and I doubt not many of them will pay up rather than be deprived of land, or they will get the Fish Curers to become security for them — Visited the Townships of Eropie, Fivepenny, KnockAird, Callicvol, Lionel, Hawbost & Swanabost to see what had been done in improving the crofts since they got the new let, but was much disappointed in seeing so little done. Visited the port of Ness & was glad to observe that they were getting large quantities of fish, some boats took yesterday upwards of 400 ling — Returned home and arrived there at 10 P.M. —

Monday 3 March

Went to the office and inspected what had been done in my absence — Went over & examined last months accounts and granted orders for their payment — Met various parties, vizt the Rev^d Mr McRae, Mr J. McDonald, Captn Burnaby, Mr J Mackenzie etc — called on Mr Munro & consulted him on various subjects — Saw Mr Howitt regarding McNabs accounts Mr Ritchie regarding works on Farms, Grounds, plantations etc — Was engaged during the evening writing letter for the Packet — arranged to take what meal we required from John Morison Sn^r at 14/- per boll out of store —

Tuesday 4 March

Had a meeting with Messrs Thomson and entered into an agreement with them for Holm Curing Houses which they take for one year from this date at a rent of £24 payable on the 15th of May next — Had a meeting with Mr Nicolson & the Banker regarding repairing of the Streets etc With the Rev^d Mr Watson Uig regarding his allowing Mr Mitchell to occupy a part of his farm Settling accounts with various contractors & retaining as much as possible off labourers for rents — Called on Mr Munro and got him to write out minute of sale between me & John McKenzie for House property — Had a meeting afterwards with J Mackenzie but did not get him to agree to all the clauses — to meet again tomorrow. Saw Bowie, Ritchie, Howitt etc on various subjects — Writing letters etc etc at office

Wednesday 5 March

Went to office and wrote letters and met various parties — Went to Parochial Meeting at 11 & was engaged there till 5 P.M. revising roll of paupers etc — Not having completed the business, adjourned to 12 o clock tomorrow — Returned to office and had meeting with Mr Alex^r Morison regarding Ground for Free Church Schools at Laxdale & Sandwick Hill — Revised Rental & Arrear lists of Parish of Uig — spent the evening with Howitt at Sandwick going over Binnies measurement and valuation of McNabs Work at Castle which I consider not to be made up in terms of agreement with McNab, and every advantage seems to be given to the Contractor —

Thursday 6 March

At office meeting parties, and writing letters, arranged various matters with Mr Ritchie as to grounds farms etc — Went to see Mr Munro about petition by Sheddens servants for aliment for themselves & Horses — Removals — some alterations in min[t]ute of sale of Houses to John Mackenzie etc etc — Attended meeting of Parochial Board to arrange general business — There was a great talk yesterday by some of the Free Church Party as to bring forward a motion against, or disapproving of the Memorial to Gov^t but I prevented the motion being brought on then till the business for which the meeting was called was first disposed of, telling them that afterwards they would have an opportunity of discussing the subject — But today they have thought better of it & let their motion fall to the ground — Steamer arrived at 4 P.M. received letters from Sir J Matheson etc Arranged with Mr Cameron for lotting remaining part of Guirshader, Examined Slip a/c for "Mary Mackenzie". Settled a/c for freight of soles etc — Was engaged till 2 A.M. with Howitt going over McNabs a/cs — My idea is that McNab himself could not have made up the account in a more favourable way for himself than Binnie has done — I am writing out objections to all the Items I consider overcharged & not in accordance with McNabs scale of prices, to send to Mr Souter — I hope a considerable reduction can be made in the a/c — Binnie should have consulted me, Howitt, or some party acting for Sir James before he made up the accounts on a one sided statement from McNab — Besides he had no power to act the part he did & on that account his valuation can be set aside —

Friday 7 March

At office meeting John McKenzie about sale of House property which we arranged finally on terms stated in my diary on 1 Feby with some additional clauses as to doing away with Byres facing Street etc — Called on Mr Munro and consulted with him about minute of sale which was signed — Had some talk with him about McNees matters he being anxious to go on with the building of the distillery — Removals etc etc — Had a call from Captⁿ Hudson & had conversation with him regarding various matters, carriage of Emigrants to Greenock, application to N. Light Ho. Comm^{rs} to get free of light dues as Steamer carries mails — Calling at Eigg with mail which the Captⁿ does not approve of — the Steamer had few passengers for the last few trips & only about half cargo — Engaged the remaining part of the day at McNabs a/c with Howitt — Adjourned to Sandwick in the evening and continued at these accounts till 4 A.M. being anxious to send them to Edin^h with my report by next Steamer — Have not so much cause to complain of measurement & valuation of wood & plaster work, as of that of masonry which is most extravagantly rated —

Saturday 8 March

At office writing letters & meeting several parties — Went over the whole rental and arrear lists of the Parish of Lochs with Mr McLeod the Ground officer and fixed on about 60 tenants to get a notice of removal who are in arrear of rent, many of them Mr McLeod thinks is able to pay up & may pay rather than be deprived of land — Those who do not can not be allowed to occupy land any longer. Prepaired list and sent same to Mr Munro to execute summonses of removal — Had talk with Brock about "Bellas" death, having suspected Munro McFarlane for certain causes, but which he thinks groundless — Thomas the Piper arrived, he is to proceed to Grimista on Monday — Had meeting with Alex^r Gair regarding payment of his a/c for salary during Mr Scobies management but could not pay it Mr Munro having arreasted the same for his creditors — Had meeting with Mr. Gair regarding Steamer — Was the remaining part of the day engaged with Howitt at McNabs a/c the examination of which I have completed, and written 152 notes of objections — Had Binnie consulted with me during the time he was going on with the measurement, or Had Mr Wilson sent me the a/cs as asked for before being closed, all this trouble would have been saved, but they avoided all intercourse or communication on the subject — Neither Mr Wilson or Mr Binnie appear to advantage in this transaction — I do not think Mr Wⁿ can have ever looked over the a/cs or he would not have allowed many items charged —

Monday 10 March

Went to office and arranged with McRae the tenant of Arinish to accept of a deduction of £10 per annum in his rent for the ground to be taken off his farm by the Lighthouse Commissioners the extent being about 6 3/4 acres, and for which the Commissioners agree to pay the proprietor a Feu duty of £12 — Saw Rod^k McKay Soval & told him Sir James was willing to assist him in emigrating to Australia, at which he seemed pleased and said he would be quite content if Sir James allowed him £40 and purchased any articles of furniture which he had & might be suitable for Soval Lodge — Had meeting with Rev^d Mr Hutchinson who wishes me to undertake the building of a cottage for him at the head of Loch Shell he having got Scotts consent — Declined taking charge of the work but offered to give him a plan, Specification, & Estimate — Purchased 40 quarters of oats from Houston for seed at 18/- — Arranged with Mr Ritchie about grass, Turnip & other seeds required for farms & ordered same Gave Howitt his instructions about proceeding to Edin^h regarding McNabs a/cs & went over several items of same with him — At office till 6 A.M. Preparing dispatches for Steamer — Sent Mr Callender McNabs a/cs with my notes on same — Also Arbiters notes in McNees case with remarks by me on notes etc —

Tuesday 11 March

At office preparing Steamer dispatches till 12 noon when she sailed — Meeting with Mr McAulay Linshader to settle a/cs — and regarding expenditure already done on his farm — Walked over Ground draining & fencing near Rope-Work & Guirshader — Examined the land as lotted at Laxdale & Guirshader by Mr Cameron — Walked along the Laxdale river & carefully examined its course for a considerable distance with the view of fixing site of Mill dam and lead for Distillery which will not be a very formidable undertaking — Examined Houses building for Widows at New Valley — Went to Castle to see works going on there in laying shewer pipes dressing up walks about Castle etc, — Went over Stables, Workshops, Byres etc — Returned to office and wrote the Ground Officers instructions about emigration, giving them all the information in my possession and asking them to send me a State shewing the quantity of clothing required in each of their districts & telling them to have the people ready by the middle of April — etc etc

Wednesday 12 March

Went to the office and had meeting with the Rev^d Mr Hutchinson & gave him plans & Specification for cottage to be built at Loch Shell by him — Meeting various parties from the Country. Arranged several matters at the office and Proceeded to Tolsta — First Inspected New Road, then went to the Store House to see meal in Store there — The fish cured here seems to be in much better order than that at Ness — Assembled the people of both Tolstas at the School House and offered the same terms as to emigration to them as what was held out to others & told them if they remained they need not look for relief from any quarter this year & that they will be expected to pay up their rent at the term — Tho' the people are very poor here & much in arrear of rent got few or none to agree to emigrate as will be seen by the following

No of Families	Souls	Arrears	Value of Stock	If Willing	
3	32	£46.12.8.	£11.10.-.	1	N. Tolsta
—	—	—	—	—	S. Tolsta

We fixed on serving 25 families with notices of removal, if they do not pay up before the term, the heads or some members of the families being fishermen — Got to Gress at 8 P.M. and remained there for the night —

Thursday 13

At Back School House met the people of Coll, Vatsker & Back and having addressed them as usual found few or none willing to emigrate, the greater part of the tenants of the two first named townships are pritty clear of arrears, and the latter being due to Mr McIver I did not insist on Emigration, more particularly as they are near good fishing ground and can always pay their rents by the Haddock fishing — We fixed on depriving 6 families in Coll of their land at Whitsunday 3 in Vatsker and 14 in Back if they do not pay up before that term — The following are those intended to emigrate —

	No of Families	Souls	Arrears	Value of Stock	If Willing
Coll	2	17	£18.10. 1.	£9.10.-.	0
Vatsker	1	8	12. 1. 7.	6.10. -.	0
Back	—	—	-. -. -.	-. -. -.	—

At Coll met the people of Tong and Aird of Tong, who also pay their rents pritty regularly — Fixed on depriving 3 families of land at Tong & the following to Emigrate

	No of Families	Souls	Arrears	Value of Stock	If Willing
Tong	1	4	£12. 0. 4.	£3. 5. 0	1
Aird of Tong	—	—	—	—	—

This round I hope will be productive of much good, shew them the necessity of excerting themselves to pay up the rent & prevent their looking to the proprietor for relief in any way —

Friday 14 March

Went to the office & had meeting with Mr Alex^r Gair regarding his a/c, Wrote Mr D Mackenzie that I did not consider Sir James entitled to pay Mr Gair his salary as charged for all the time he remained idle here, that Sir James wrote him in 1849 that he did not require his services after Mart^s &

that whoever was the cause of the delay must be liable — Wrote J. McDonald ground officer Uig in reply to his letter asking for food for some of those who are to emigrate & who are now destitute, that he may set them to work at roads & give them Destitution Meal — Went to Justice of Pease Court to see Poachers tried for fishing, four were found guilty and fined failing payment thereof to be imprisoned — Attended meeting of Water Co^y, but there not being a quorum did not get on with the business — Had meeting with Mr Munro on various subjects — Went to the office & meet the Sheriff, Mrs Lees, Houston, Inspector of Uig poor, Contractors etc — Examined and settled John McFarquhars a/cs for Smith work for Home, Sand^k Hill & Holm Farms — Went over various a/cs & granted orders for payment of same — A Brig loaded with coals went down in the Broad Bay today Crew saved —

Saturday 15 March

Went to the office and examined the Paybills for grounds & Home farm for work done during the last three months, sent Mr Morison to Distillery to pay the same and to retain as much as possible for rents — Gave list of arrears of Feu duty to George McLeod with instructions to call on all due & ask them to pay or that they will be prosecuted — Had meetings with various parties Mr Gerrie, Mr Clark several Contractors etc — Went to Castle and walked over same, an accident nearly took place with the gas in the still room a few nights ago — Walked over the grounds & gardin with Mr Ritchie and arranged several matters to be done — examined square, offices, workshops etc and gave Bowie a lecture about not keeping things more tidy. Returned to office and was engaged taking evidence regarding some of McRae Arinish Sheep said to be killed by Brocks dogs — Writing letters, meeting parties etc — Gave instructions to Bowie & McIntosh Holm to begin planting potatoes & prepare for sowing oats —

Monday 17 March

Went to Garabost and inspected the tile work which is now doing very well and turning out a large quantity of tiles, the weather being favourable, and the work in good order — Met the people of Port Naguran, Aird, Port Vollar, Seshader & Sulishader — Addressed them on the subject of Emigration, and put the offer of a free passage etc within their reach, told them that if they remained they need not look to the proprietor for relief in food, seed corn, or employment and that they would be expected to pay up their rents on the term day, otherwise they would be deprived of their holdings — Got none in these townships to agree to emigrate, but fixed on the following to be deprived of their lands

	No of Families	Amount of Arrears	Average of each
Port Naguran	2	£ 7.19.11	£ 3. 19.11.1/2
Port Vollar	1	11.11. 5.	11.11. 5.
Aird	5	35. 9. 1.	7. 1. 9.3/4
Seshader	5	58. 3. 7.	11.12. 8.3/4
Sulishader	2	13.17. 4.	6.18. 8.

The people of these townships are all fishermen & ought to have had their rents paid up, but several of the above are desparate characters that must be made an example of — Got home at 10 P.M.

Tuesday 18 March

Went to office and met several people arranged various matters, wrote letters — Proceeded to Garabost and met the people of that township, Upper and Lower Bayble, Knock, Swordale, Melbost & Branahui, addressed them as usual on Emigration, more punctual payment of rents if they remained, and warned them that they need not look for any extrenuous relief — no families agreed to emigrate, but we fixed on depriving the following of their holdings at [*no date shown in diary*]

	No of Families	Amount of Arrears	Average to each family
Garabost	4	£ 25.11. 8	£ 6. 7.11.
Upper Bayble	14	126. 4. 3.	9. 0. 3.1/2
Lower Bayble	11	98.12.10	8.19. 4.
Knock	4	33. 5. 9.	8. 6. 5.1/4
Swordale	5	53.18. 9.	10.15. 9.
Melbost	2	13. 8. 11.	6.14. 5.1/2
Branahui	3	18. 6. -.	6. 2. -.

I have no doubt but a large proportion of the above will pay up their arrears rather than be deprived of their lands, and if they do so they may be allowed to remain — they have a right to a way going crop at all events, and the greater number promise to pay up before it is removed from the ground — Had Mr Morison with me & settled with the work people at the Brick Work retaining the greater part of their wages for rent — Dined at the Free Manse & there met the Rev^d McGrigor. Returned to the Brick Work and finished my business there — Got home at 11 P.M. Wrote Mr Munro regarding removals in the Parishes of Lochs & Barvas, also to Mr McDonald Ness and Mr McLeod Valtos. An officer is already gone to Uig

Wednesday 19 March

Went to Melbost Carse to see the Farmers' Society's ploughing match where there were 14 ploughs at Work   John Nicolson who took the first prize last year was again successful today — The prise for the Best Sample of Bear weighing 53 lb per bushel was awarded to the Lodge Farm, for the best sample of oats which weighed 43 lb per bushel to Alexander Aignish — For the best field of turnips to Alexander Aignish, second best to Sandwick — Went to Stornoway & called at the Gas Work & patent Slip, gave foreman directions on various matters, examined account for dues etc of schooner "Exile" to be launched this evening — Went to office & wrote letters to several parties — Mr Munro as to recovery of feu duties, Ground officers regarding protection of oyster beds etc — Going over rentals of House property in Stornoway & asking for payment — Meeting parties vizt Mr P Clark, Mr R Mackenzie, Mr J. Morison and Country people — Dined at the Lews Hotel with the Farmers Society which went off very well & was respectably attended —

Thursday 20th March

Went to the office and met the Inspector of the parish of Lochs regarding a Lunatic a native of that Parish who is to be sent to the Glasgow Asylum — Mr McLeod Valtos regarding Emigration etc — Captn of vessel sunk in Broad Bay — went with him to Mr R Morison and arranged to supply his men with the necessary articles of clothing & expence of boarding here to be paid by the Shipwrecked Fishermen & Mariners Socty — Walked over ground behind Inaclate with Mr Cameron & fixed how it was to be lotted — Went to Melbost Farm House & there met the people of Stainish — Sandwick Hill, Lower Sandwick, Holm, Coulnagrean & Gariscore — 3 families agreed to emigrate, and we arranged to deprive the following numbers in each Township of their land —

	No of Families	Amount of Arrears	Average arrears of each
Stainish	6	£ 65. 8.10.	£10.18. 1.1/2
Sandk Hill	7	13.10.10.	1.18. 8.
Lower Sandk	21	102.14. 6.	4.17.10.
Holm	3	20. 3. 3.	6.14. 5.
Coulnagrean	2	7.10. 9.	3.15. 4.1/2

Steamer arrived received letters from Sir James — Had a call from the Revd Mr McRae & had some talk on the Glebe Case — The Presbytery is to meet on Wednesday first to take up the business — He wants the part of the ground for new glebe not drained to be drained & to be exempted from water rates for the cottage, on the ground that he has water free of cost at Tong or that, if the money allowance is increased to £40 the Presbytery will be content with matters as they are — I told him we had arranged all already & that he had pledged himself to stand to that arrangement — which he said was the case —

Friday 21 March

Had meeting with Mr E McIver who arrived yesterday by the Steamer — He seems quite willing to agree to Sir James proposal not to expend the £500 on Gress this year — but would wish to expend about £100 on Sheep draining — He has arranged with Mr Hutchinson Glasgow to send the Skye boat to Loch Inver & guarantees £30 per trip between Loch Inver & intermediate ports — Went to Steamer which has had a full cargo this trip, but a considerable quantity for the owner — Went to office and arranged various matters & met several parties — Went to Laxdale & met the people of Guirshader, Laxdale & Old Markethill — Went over their a/cs, offered those behind, the same terms in regard to Emigration as in other parts of the Country but got none to go — Fixed on removing 14 families their agrigate arrears being £88.4.8. Thereafter walked over the ground & valued the same along with Mr Cameron, and relet it to the parties who had paid up their rent — There are 30 lots, the annual rental being £54.11.5. — this land is in a very bad state, more than a third of it has never been reclaimed —

Saturday 22 March

Went to the office and revised conditions of let for Goathill Parks — Met several parties viz Mr Nov. McIver, Mrs Watson, Mr Ritchie, Country people etc — Went to Goathill to let the Parks & having set them all up to auction one after another, did not get an offer of more than 20/- per acre for them, on that account did not let any except three to tradespeople at the old rents — I have no doubt but I can get them all let yet at nearly the old rents, there being a sort of combination today to get the rents reduced — Returned to the office & examined several witnesses regarding the killing of Sheep on Arinish farm said to be by Brocks dogs, but there is no direct proof Had meeting with Alexander Aignish regarding his farm, he offered to increase his offer to £110 if the Steading was put in order for him, I said I would rather recommend to Sir James to reduce the rent asked from £100 to £90 on condition that the tenant repaired the Steading & maintained it during his lease, and asked no outlay on the part of the Landlord, except supplying him with some brick with which the tenant was to build at his own expence cattle shed — where & as may be agreed on — Alexander agrees to this proposal if confirmed by Sir James —

Monday 24 March

Went to office and was engaged meeting parties viz Mr Gair regarding Steamer arrangements & a/cs — Mr Munro regarding removals, Rev^d Mr Watson regarding claim for damages for not clearing his farm of Mr Mitchell & small tenants at Whitsunday last, tho' he agreed and wished to accommodate Mitchell — Got him to sign a Minute drawn up by Mr Munro agreeing to withdrawing his claim & promised to give him the small place of Mavaig which lies into his farm, there are three small tenants here at present occupying it who can be removed to Carishader in place of those going to America — Attended a meeting of the Gas & Water Co^y — Went to Steamer to arrange various matters with the Captn — Writing dispatches till 3 A.M.

Tuesday 25 March

At office writing dispatches for Steamer till 12 noon — Went by Steamer to Loch Schell, landed at Lemervay and took boat to Stemervay where I met the Rev^d Mr Hutchinson at the cottage, which is in a bad state of repair, and seems never to have been well finished — The floors in both rooms are very bad being very uneven & composed of clay & rock — agreed to board both rooms & line on[e] of them with wood, put in fixed beds, & put up a small place at the end of the cottage for dogs, the whole work not to exceed £15 to £20 — This cottage is not at Ieskine for which place (two miles distant) we took boat — Parted there with Mr Hutchinson, walked to Habost six miles over the moor & crossed Loch Eerisord to Valtos where I remained for the night — Saw a number of moor fowl as I went along —

Wednesday 26 March

Took boat to Laxay where I met a number of people, some wishing to emigrate & others who have got notice of removal — Proceeded to Stornoway called at the Castle and told Mrs Watson to have rooms ready to receive Sir John McNeill by tomorrow — Meet various parties at office — Attended Meeting of Presbytery regarding Glebe Case, where it was arranged that Mr McRae & I should come before the Presbytery as pititioners, adjourned till tomorrow till pitition is drawn up which Mr Munro undertakes. The "Comet" having come into the harbour, left the meeting before the business was closed, and went on board of her to call for Sir John McNeill who I found very frank, he told me what he had been doing elsewhere, & how he intended to proceed here — I asked him on shore & told him there were rooms ready for his accommodation at the Castle, he seemed rather to hesitate, saying he was certain he would be more comfortable on shore, but feared it would not look well to live at the Castle, however he would dine there tomorrow — He took a room at the Hotel where he was to be seen by all parties & take evidence. I offered him every assistance in my power, but he said it would not do for him to appear to be laid [*sic*] by me in any way — to which I replied that I was at his service when he wanted me — Went to the Castle & arranged with Mrs Watson to get dinner ready for Sir John tomorrow, & sent on board some fresh provisions — Had meeting with Mr E McIver and arranged to have the Gress House & offices inspected by Howitt & Alex^r McKenzie Jn^r to see that it was left in proper & good repair as stated in lease ordinary tear & wear excepted — He gave me a letter stating that he would be content with an expenditure of £100 this year on Gress, an increase in proportion to be made on the present rent, with interest of money laid out — At office writing letters —

Thursday 27 March

Sir John McNeill is at the Lews Hotel examining parties and giving interviews to all who call on him — At office meeting and arranging with parties who are to Emigrate — Attended meeting of Presbytery and agreed to the prayer of Mr McRae's pitition which was laid on the table till next meeting, which is called for this day fortnight and at which all concerned are to get notice to attend for their interests — Asked the members of Presbytery to meet Sir John at dinner this evening at the Castle — Mr Munro the Sheriff & Captn Burnaby — Went to the Castle and gave out the plate and wine — Returned to the office and went over the a/cs of the month and granted orders for payment — Went to the Castle to meet Sir John his secretary Mr Peterkin etc etc   Mrs Watson managed everything remarkably well —

Friday 28 March

Meeting Parties at the office and writing letters till 12 — Attended meeting of the four Parochial boards of the Island called by Sir John who gave an address stating the cause for his calling the meeting, explained the nature and obligations of the existing poor Act for Scotland, that no able bodied person was entitled to relief, but if such a person was entirely destitute and without the means of support in a day or two he & his family would be reduced by want, & legally come on the board for support and in that way it came to be a question with the boards whether they would give such a person assistance before his health was injured by starvation or wait till he had a legal claim — He recommended that they should give relief in the first case, but not while the applicant had property of any kind. He then put three questions to each member of each board —

1   Do you know of any person who died of want, or any person whoes [*sic*] health has been injured from want of food? Answered in the negative by all —

2   Do you think there will be destitution & is there a danger of parties suffering for want of food before next crop if not assisted? Answered yes by all except by Mr John Morison Sn^r & a few others

3   Do the Parochial Boards order their Inspectors to grant assistance to all destitute persons to prevent a loss of life? Agreed to by the Boards

— Several questions were put to Sir John by members of the Boards which he answered satisfactorily — The meeting then separated — Thereafter Mr Peterkin had a meeting with the officers of the Boards to inspect their books and proceedings — gave them instructions on various points — and found fault with all for not keeping a register of the paupers — At office meeting people from the Country regarding payment of rents, removals Emigration etc — Prevailed on Sir John to remain at the Castle and invited to dine with him the Rev^d Mr Campbell Uig, Drs Millar McRae & McLeod, Mr Youll & Dr Monteith of the "Comet" The Banker Mr J R McIver, Mr McAulay Linshader & Mr Cameron — Sir John seemed anxious to meet with the most respectable and intelligent to know their views & hear what they had to say so I thought it proper to give as many as possible an opportunity of meeting him — Arranged with Sir John as to his visitation of the Country Parishes

Saturday 29 March

Went to the Castle according to appointment and was examined by Sir John on the State of the Country & the people, What had been done & is doing by the proprietor — The rents charged, the quantity of land in each lot, the quantity of moor grazings attached to each township etc etc Accompanied Sir John to the Point District, Called to see the Brick work, where he held a meeting with the Constables of all the Townships in the district — Asked them the rents paid, what quantity of land had they in cultivation, what number of cattle, sheep & horses had they & what were they allowed to keep, what they sowed & what returns they got etc etc All the answers from each he took down in writing — The Constables gave a true statement of how things stood, and told how much the Proprietor had done for them etc, Sir John seemed much pleased with them, and told them they need not look for relief from any quarter whatever. The Gov^t. could do nothing, the Dest. Com^{ee} had expended their funds, & the Proprietor who had done so much already, more than any proprietor he knew, could not be expected to go on laying out money on unprofitable works — Went with him to Bayble, Shader etc and shewed him what was doing on the crofts in which he seemed to take an interest —
Sir John again resumed my examination in the evening which lasted till 3 A.M. being anxious to complete it before going to the Country — Arranged matters with Mrs Watson for tomorrow etc etc

Monday 31 March

Started for Barvas accompanied by Sir John McNeill & Mr Peterkin, went as far as Shader to See the ground reclaimed there and now given to small tenants, also land now being improved by the tenants — Sir John walked over the land and conversed with the people asking them the returns they had from their land, the amount of rents, cost of improving etc, he thought well of these people and considered them in comparatively prosperous condition — Returned to the Manse of Barvas where he took the Rev^d Mr McRae's declaration as to the state of the Country, and the changes that have taken place for the last 40 years. Mr McRae stated that when he came to the Parish he found the people well off having plenty of cattle sheep & money, and that he would have lent parties then £5 more readily than he would now lend 5/- — The cause of the present poverty of the people he assigns to the subdivition of the lots — The fall in the price of kelp & black Cattle — Stopping the distillation of whisky — and latterly the failure of the potatoe crop — Mr McRae thinks no small tenant should have less than 10 acres of land; but being asked by Sir John if there were any in the Parish who would take such lots & were able to stock them answered that he did not know of any — Being asked what it would take to Stock a 10 acre lot and maintain a family till the first crop was taken off it answered (after making an Estimate) £100 — Being asked if he knew any in the Parish who could command such a sum, said he knew not one — Sir John held a conversation with, and examined several of the Constables of Upper & Lower Barvas — Told them they need not look for support from any quarter etc etc — Proceeded to Shawbost and meet the constables of Arnold, North & South Bragar, North & South Shawbost. Sir John asked them various questions about their state & circumstances, if they were now destitute, if they had seed etc etc — Warned them not to expect help from any quarter whatever, and pointed out to them how much was already done, and that they were now worse off than ever — Examined John McDonald who had taken a lot of 10 acres two years ago — last year he gave up two acres of it, and this year he has given up four more, now retaining only 4 acres, the cause was that he found he could not pay the rent & had not capital to purchase stock for such a large lot — Sir John seemed pleased to get such evidence as he said the great cry was "give the people more land" which he thinks does more harm than good if they have no capital to buy stock by which they must pay their rents — Walked over the land improved at Shawbost and let to the people, Angus McAulay also took a lot of 10 acres but this year has given up the half of it as he found he could not pay his rent — Proceeded to Dalbeg Inn where we remained for the night —

Tuesday 22 April

...nt to office and was engaged meet...
...rious parties from the Country rega...
...migration &c – Had meeting with the...
...Mc Gregor regarding Certain Rules h...
...wished to be adopted in the man...
...ent of the Industrial School, a...
...hich I promised to lay before his...
...his Lady for their approval if...
...withdrew one which I considere...
...open – and which he agreed to...
...ttling Accounts with Govern & th...
...nson Mossens for work done...
...their farms – Writing letters – Arran...
...a supplying emigrants with Clothi...
...examined tax &c and paid San...
...ent to Castle to see his Ennis...
...d not find him at home –
...turned to office and met num...
...people from the Country on v...
...matters — Had meeting with Rod...

Tuesday 1 April

Started for Carloway at 10 o'clock, called for Mr Kenneth Ross the Free Church Cathicist, got him to accompany us to Humphreys where he was placed under examination by Sir John McNeill but I was not present at the examination — Thereafter took boat at Loch Carloway, Mr John McDonald having come to meet us with his boat, proceeded to the Sound of Barnera where we landed and met the Constables of the Island. Sir John made his usual enquiries and afterwards addressed the people telling them they need not look from aid from any quarter — One man stood up and spoke against emigration, and said he had got a summons of removal, but would not go to America. Sir John recommended emigration, and asked him what he would do in this Country when he acknowledged he had neither seed to put in the ground nor food to support himself & Family to which he answered that if he had land he could support them — Sir John asked him if his land would yield any food before harvast and how did he mean to support his family during the interval but this he could not answer — took an early dinner with John McDonald and set sail for Valtos where we arrived after a hard battle with a head wind & tide, had the boat not been a good one, & well manned we could not have crossed Loch Roag it having come on a gale of wind — Sir John held a meeting in the Valtos School House with the people of that township and Kneep, asked them the usual questions & addressed them as in other places — He told me that he had got very alarming information as to the State of the people in these townships, but that he saw nothing to fear — He examined me at great length as to the removals from these townships, about which he seemed to have got incorrect information — From Valtos walked to the Manse of Uig amid a storm of wind & rain, where we arrived at 7 P.M. quite drenched—

Wednesday 2 April

Sir John was engaged during the forenoon examining John McDonald the Ground Officer, who stated the condition of the people as very destitute — But at same time the idleness of the people, the difficulty of getting them to work, the works carried on by the Proprietor in the parish such as Road Making & improvements on crofts, the latter of which was suspended as the people could not be got to go on with the work — etc etc — Sir John met the Constables and people of the upper end of the Parish which are the most destitute in Lews & which he pronounced to be the most miserable people he had yet seen — Many of them are quite destitute & desparate and are now supported by the Charity of their neighbours — When starvation comes on one it will come on all — Sir John put his usual questions as to what rent they paid, what stock they had, what they sowed & what returns they had — The greater part of the rent in this district is placed on the pasture land so that the rents appear high as the arable land is very limited, and they have little or no stock on the pasture, so that they cannot be expected to pay full rents having nothing to meet them — This district cannot support its population without potatoes so that the sooner it is cleared the better — Left the Manse at 3 P.M. walked to Meavag & took boat for Callanish were we dined & afterwards, proceeded to Stornoway arrived at the Castle at 10 P.M. and after taking a rest & cup of tea Sir John went on board the "Comet" at 12 to be ready to Start early in the morning — Sir John purchased a Lews cow at Callanish as a present for his daughter being the smallest he ever saw — Sir John seemed pleased at the attention shewn him —

Thursday 3 April

At office reading over and answering letters which arrived in my absence — Preparing information for Sir John McNeill — Going over monthly accounts & granting order for payment of same — Looked over Cash book for last month — Had meeting with Gerrie regarding complesion of the Uig Road — With Mr Ritchie regarding articles purchased at Sheddens Sale amounting to £71 which will cover the years rent — Called on Mr Munro but did not find him in — Went to the Castle to arrange various matters with Mrs Watson — Steamer arrived, received dispatches, several lettters from Sir James who delays coming till the 17th — A pair of Rabbits and three ducks arrived by the Steamer for the Castle, one of the ducks having died on the passage — Returned to the office and had meeting with John Morison, Mr McDonald etc etc

Friday 4 April

Called on Mr Munro and consulted him on various subjects arranged to meet again in the afternoon — Was engaged meeting parties viz Mr J. Morison, Contractors and various Country people in regard to Emigration. Went to Steamer and arranged for Carriage of furniture to Castle, the articles liable to breakage in carriage being left behind in Glasgow, what came just now is being carted, great care being used in putting the articles into the carts which are ordered to go by the New Road to prevent damage, seven articles were landed broken from the Steamer — Met Mr Munro & went over (with him) the Glebe papers sent from Edin^h also the Model feu Charter and Opinion — Sheddens a/cs etc etc — Examined Sallary a/cs and granted orders for payment of same — Writing letters to various parties etc —

Saturday 5 April

Went to office and settled several of Mr Scobies a/cs vizt Matheson for work done by him at Dalbeg House & Borve School — Murray & McArthurs a/c for Smith Work — Paid Mr W^m McKay & Mr Grant Mr Scobies clerks their salaries — Got a State of debts due by John McKay up to this date amounting to £21 for which I gave cash to his brother William to pay off being £14 more than was due him for salary. W^m is to buy all he requires after this and lay out his money to the best advantage. Had meeting with the Banker regarding settlement with him of a/c due under Mr Scobies management, wrote Donald McKenzie to meet the Banker & J. R. MacIver in my office on Wednesday to endeavour to settle these a/cs — Donald refused to come the last day I wrote him till he got orders from Edin^h which he has now got — Attended meeting of the Inhabitants called in the Mason Hall by the Stornoway Merchants to oppose emigration on the grounds that if the people were sent to America they would lose their debts which they have against them — Mr John Morison Sn^r who was the most active person in getting up the meeting was called to the Chair. He made several speeches stating many untruths & misrepresenting matters, which were met by statements of facts & arguments from me & Mr Munro — Mr J R Mackenzie also spoke in a most violent manner and made several misstatements several of which I was able to contradict & which he seemed to withdraw & cooled down — Several persons addressed the meeting against Emigration & others not against emigration, but against sending away people who were in their debt — The question of rents was discussed — The meeting resolved to detain all who were in debt to them — and represented Sir James kind offer of sending so many free to America as tyranical & cruel — And a breach of his pledge at the Parochial Board that he would not compel people to Emigrate — I stated that no one c^d compel the people to emigrate, and that they need not go unless they please, but that all those who were in arrear for rent two years & upwards, would be deprived of their land at Whitsunday next if not paid up by then, giving them the option of emigrating if they can not pay — That the proprietor can do with his land as he pleases and that other parties have no right to interfere or dictate to him what he is to do — That those who do not pay their rents cannot be allowed to remain in possession of lands — Returned to the office & arranged various matters with Alexander, Houston etc etc. The merchants did not seem pleased at the result of the meeting they thought they could carry all their own way —

7 April 1851

Went to the office and was engaged there all day going over last months a/c, valuation of stock on hand at end of year, and accounts outstanding for seeds Cattle etc — Preparing answers to queries from Free Church Com^ee 51 in number — Called on Mr Munro to consult him on various subjects — Writing dispatches for Steamer till 3 A.M. —

Tuesday 8 April

At office preparing dispatches for Steamer till 12 noon when she sailed — Gave instructions to Mr Ritchie as to preparing Plans & Specification for New Glebe & Manse offices — Called on Mr Munro. Meeting various parties from the Country Going over and preparing statement of Sheddens a/cs — arranged with Thomas McKay about taking charge of Grimista & Black Water Rivers —

Wednesday 9 April

Went to Court House being cited as a juryman but after waiting the whole forenoon got off not being ballotted — Two person[s] from Uig were tried & found guilty of Sheep Stealing & sentenced one to 2 months & the other to 3 months imprissonment — Went to office and met various parties from the Country — Was the remaining part of the day engaged with Mr D Mackenzie settling accounts with the Banker — extending from 1844 to 1848 — Called on Mr Munro with Alexander Aignes and instructed him as to the terms of our agreement in order that a Missive of lease may be made out —

Thursday 10th April

Went to office and was engaged meeting parties, Mr Alex^r McLeod the Lochs Ground Officer regarding people emigrating from his district, gave him instructions to go on with making kelp @ 40/- per ton — Gave him my answers to the Free Church Com^ee's Queries that he might See the Rev^d Mr Finlayson & Allan Ross on the subject — Arranged with Mr Cameron & John Mackenzie about beginning to take delivery of Emigrants Stocks — Meeting various people from the Country regarding Emigration etc — Attended meeting of Presbytery regarding Glebe Case where a number of the feuers appeared and on being told that no part of the expense of additions to Goathill Cottage offices & Glebe fence was to be exacted from them, they seemed satisfied and thought the excambion would be favourable to all parties — Got an adjournment of the Presbytery till we can have advice from Edin^h and the plans are completed — Mr McRae gave a long and contradictory address to the Presbytery blaming Sir James for having caused such delay (or rather his agents) for he always thought Sir James intended & wished to do what was right — But the change was of little good to him now as he had lost the greater part of his congregation and might be prevented for years from enjoying the change as all depended on Captn Burnabys leaving the Country which might not take place for years. He then went over the old arguments for the old Glebe at Tong & Common pasture, and in fact seemed to me to be using every argument in his power to prejudise the other members of Presbytery against the new arrangement saying the privileges offered were in no way equal to those now possessed. I made a few remarks in way of answer, (1) that the presbytery was alone to blame for the delay & not carrying out the first arrangement, having delayed or refused to give Mr McLeod Kingsburgh the powers required by him — (2) that Mr McRae had pledged himself to be satisfied with the proposal now before the Presbytery and had in fact pititioned the presbytery to sanction it, and that I could not but be surprised at his remarks, (3) that if he shifted his ground a hair breadth I considered himself as free from the arrangement, that I had power from Sir James to carry out the arrangment so far as already agreed to but if Mr McRae or the Presbytery imposed any new conditions I considered the matter at an end — To which Mr McRae replied that he was satisfied with the arrangement — Several members of the presbytery stated that the matter could not now be dropped, but they must go on with it — The Presbytery then adjourned — Went to the office and was the whole of the remaining part of the day settling & arranging matters with the Banker connected with Mr Scobies a/cs —

Friday 11 April

Came to a final Settlement with the Banker & got a discharge from him there being a balance of £666.14.4. in his favour — Engaged during the whole day settling with Contractors for Works done & retaining as much as possible for arrears of rent etc — Wrote letters to various parties — Walked over Sand^k Hill with McIntosh to see what crop was laid down

Saturday 12 April

At office settling with Contractors & writing letters — Meeting various parties & granted orders for seed potatoes etc — Went to Patent Slip & inspected same, gave directions on various matters — Walked with Mr Ritchie over land now being laid down under crop at Bayhead, Guirshader & new Garden — also inspected fences building — Walked over grounds & saw what the people were about — Thereafter went over the Castle,

Stables, & office Houses. Returned to the office & received letters & papers by the Packet—

Monday 14 April

Went to office and was engaged meeting parties, granting orders for seed potatoes, writing letters for packet, and making up information for Sir John McNeill as to land improvements & Emigration. Writing Ground Officers on various subjects—Going over Accounts and granting orders for payment of same —

Tuesday 15 April

Called on Mr Munro and there met Urquhart and his agent Wm Munro, had some talk with them about disputed Items in the Accounts — Got from Mr Munro deposit receipt in favour of Duncan Montgomery Balallan. Wrote Mr McLeod for information regarding his proper & lawful heir there being two claimants — At office writing letters to various parties — Had a long meeting with Mr J .R. McIver regarding his a/cs with Mr Scobie but came to no settlement, there being a difference almost in every item — Fixed to meet again tomorrow & wrote Mr D Mackenzie to attend — Went over the whole of Sheddens accounts & gave state of same to Mr Munro — Meeting various parties from the Country — Went to the Castle and arranged with Mrs Watson & Bowie to prepare for Sir James & Lady Mathesons arrival tomorrow evening —

Wednesday 16 April

Went to office and was engaged meeting parties, writing letters and settling a/cs — Going over & examining Sheddens a/cs etc. Attended meeting of Parochial Board of Stornoway, fixed the assessment at 2/6 per pound for the ensuing year & instructed the Inspector to make up the Ass[ess]ment Roll — Had a long discussion on giving relief to the able bodied, but delayed coming to a decision, the meeting being but poorly attended — adjourned till Friday — Called on Mr Munro & arranged to pitition the Sheriff to appoint compitent persons to inspect & value work done by Shedden & part of his contracts not completed — Engaged till past 8 o'clock with Mr James R McIver & Donald McKenzie arranging accounts incurred during Mr Scobies management, there were great difficulties & differences at starting but reduced the balance to a difference of £12 — Steamer arrived at 1/2 past 9 with Sir James & Lady Matheson on board — Went to the Castle —

Thursday 17 April

Went to the office and had meeting with Mr Scott who has come here to see site of Light House, Quarries etc with a view to offer for building it, gave him all the information I was in possession of and sent my brother with him to point out the ground etc — Went over pitition regarding Sheddens Works with Mr Munro — Went to Steamer to arrange about her sailing at 4 tomorrow and sending notice regarding Scotts Sheep etc — Went to Castle to call for Sir James, gave out wine — Had some talk with Sir James about Emigration etc — He wishes me to write to engage another vessel — Walked with him to Creed — Went to office & wrote dispatches for Steamer — Returned to the Castle at Sir James request — Prepared answers to queries by the Free Church Presbytery regarding Emigration etc —

Friday 18 April

Breakfasted at the Castle, and was present at interview with Free Church Presbytery — Read answers to their queries, at which with other explanations they seemed satisfied at least expressed themselves so — Accompanied Sir James to meeting of Parochial Board where several hours were spent in discussing the subject of granting relief to able bodied who are utterly destitute of food & means — The Inspector was directed after due inquiry to grant relief to such — But to get work done for any relief granted & to relieve none who had anything of their own till they first disposed of such property — Went to office & finished dispatches for Steamer & saw her off at 1/2 past 4 — Accompanied Sir James to Bayhead round by the Rope Work, Goathill & Guirshader to see land improvements & progress made in removing Bayhead people — Returned to the office & arranged various matters etc —

Saturday 19 April

Went to office and had meeting with the Banker regarding Wm Morisons & Co^y a/cs for Steamers & for wool purchased from the Estate — With Mr Munro regarding various matters — Wrote letters to severals — Went to Castle to see Sir James, inspected old house behind Castle with the view of altering it, but the expence (£150) being considered rather too much Sir James ordered it to be merely repaired in the mean time & the West Wing to be removed, this house is to be converted into a dairy & Milking House. Received orders to go on with the erection of a stable & Coach House at Morskill — Returned to office and met several Country people regarding emigration etc — Packet arrived at 3 P.M. — going over rental a/cs for Poor Law Ass^t etc etc.

Monday 21

Called on Mr Munro regarding the punishment of poachers — Glebe Case etc etc — Had meeting with the Banker and settled dispute regarding wool purchased by his son, the sum agreed to be paid by him is £115 odds — of which he paid £61 — met Mr D Mackenzie & Peter McFarlane regarding the a/c of the latter, and after spending some hours with them could not get them to come to a settlement — Looked over goods got for Emigrants & placed them under the charge of Mr A McIver — Settled a/cs for cattle with Mr McAulay Linshader. Went to Castle to see Sir James. Had conversation regarding Steamers & Emigrant Ships, when it was arranged to charter other two of the same size as the "Barlow" — At office writing letters for the Packet. Arranged sailing days for Steamer with Mr Gair in the event of her not being sold & sent note of same to Mr I. E. Matheson — Had meeting with the Rev^d Mr McGrigor regarding School examination, emigration, answers to Free Church Queries etc — Saw various Country people regarding Emigration etc —

Tuesday 22 April

Went to office and was engaged meeting various parties from the Country regarding Emigration etc — Had meeting with the Rev^d Mr McGrigor regarding certain rules which he wished to be adopted in the management of the Industrial School, and which I promised to lay before Sir James & his Lady for their approval if he withdrew one which I considered improper — and which he agreed to do — Settling accounts with Gerrie & McPherson Mossend for work done on their farms — Writing letters — Arranging for supplying emigrants with clothing — Examined tax a/cs and paid same — Went to Castle to see Sir James but did not find him at home — Returned to office and met numbers of people from the Country on various matters — Had meeting with Rod^k McKay & told him Sir James would pay £40 to 50 to a/c of his passage money

Wednesday 23

Went to the office and arranged several matters with Mr Morison — Had meeting with Collector Jeffreys regarding his inspection of Emigrant ships — met various parties from the Country. Attended examination of Industrial School by the Free Church Presbytery. The School seemed to be in a very Satisfactory state and the Examinators well pleased — Thereafter had meetings with various parties who are to emigrate, and went to the shop to see how matters were going on — Returned to office and examined several a/c and expenditure of this month to this date — Wrote answers to queries by Sir James as to quantity of bread stuffs consumed by a working man & his family etc — Called at Castle but did not see Sir James. Walked over part of grounds — Returned to office & wrote to Sir James with State of Bank a/c, Note of Expenditure this month etc — Wrote each Ground Officer to remove houses occupied by emigrants so soon as they leave etc

Thursday 24

Went to office and read letters received by the Steamer & Packet, Met various parties from the Country who intend to Emigrate — gave instructions for supplying them with clothing etc — Went to the Castle and had consultation with Sir James regarding sale of Steamers & Ships for Emigrants — Followed Mr Spooner to the Whin Park and accompanied him over the Ground improved at Guirshader, Bayhead & Goathill. Went to office and met Sir James regarding agreement to be entered into with the owners of the steamer "Islay" for supplying the Lews with steam Communication. Wrote letters for Packet — Met various parties from the Country, Emigrants etc — Accompanied Mr Spooner over land drained behind Inaclate, Also at Sandwick & Mossend — Returned to the office and arranged various matters —

Friday 25

At office meeting parties who intend to Emigrate and arranging matters with them — Went over Nisbets a/c for Ironmongery with him — Had a call from Mr Spooner and had conversation on several subjects with him — Had meetings with various parties vizt Mr Nicolson, Mr Alex^r Morison, Rev^d Mr McGrigor, Mr Alexander, Mr J. Morison, etc etc — Settling accounts with various parties & writing letters — Went to Goathill to meet Mr Spooner, followed him to Laxdale, thence to the Castle — Called on Sir James, consulted him about letting Scaliscro to John Mitchell, but he would prefer continuing it with the McRaes if a proper arrangement could be made, which is not very easy, seeing that their stock could not be kept off the forest, and there would be a constant traffic between Scaliscro and Kean Reasort, and the moor between occupied by their sheep, besides the McRaes have enough in Reef and Ken Reasort, and Mitchell is a respectable young man with a little means & has no holding — Also consulted about letting fields now occupied by Mr McIver in Goathill to Mr Gerrie allowing him to repair or rebuild the fences @ 6d per yard payable out of first years rent — He offers £18 per annum but must come up to £20 — Consulted as to term of the Rev^d Mr McRaes entry to the Cottage — Cash Matters etc etc—

Saturday 26 April

Called on Mr Munro and arranged with him to draw up form of agreement to be entered into with owners of Steamer "Islay" for carrying on the trade to this port — from notes given by Sir James — Met various parties at the office — Went to the Castle & spent some time with Mr Spooner regarding drainage works, farms, etc.   Accompanied Sir James with Mr Nisbet over part of the House to measure windows for blinds etc — John Mitchell called to see Sir James regarding Scaliscro Farm — Miss McIver called regarding some new arrangements proposed by Rev^d Mr McGrigor in her School, Sir James advised her not to oppose his wishes to withdraw the children from her School on Sunday & send them to the Free Church — Arranged Cash Matters with Sir James & got £1000 in R B Bank notes & £1100 in cheques — Returned to office & settled with Mr Nisbet — Told John Mitchell that he would get the lower part of Scaliscro at £45 and if the March was shifted to the Road @ £50 to give him a vote — but that I would write confirming this arrangement when I had consulted with Sir James.   Arranged various matters, & wrote letters to several parties —

Monday 28 April

Went to office and wrote letters to various parties — Had conversation with Mr Cameron regarding Emigration & taking stock from those leaving — Had meeting with Mr Munro regarding minute of agreement to be entered into with owners of steamer "Islay" etc — Engaged the greater part of the day with Mr Gair examining Steamer a/cs which for repairs continue extravagant — Settled with Christie for building of safe — Met various Emigrants & arranged with John McKenzie to give them work for Des^t Meal at Shawbost & Barvas — Went to Castle & consulted Sir James on various subjects, proposed going to Glasgow to settle steamer arrangements — Saw Mr Spooner & talked over various matters — Went to Steamer office & asked Mr Gair to prepare statements shewing traffic for each year etc

Tuesday 29 April 1851

At office all day making arrangements for leaving the Country, going over a/cs and granting orders for payment of same, Writing letters to various parties and preparing despatches for Steamer — Sir James called at office & laid before him State shewing outstanding freights and liabilities for Steamers, the former amounting to £1942.7/- including £984.5.7. payable by the owner & the latter amounting to £2618.19.3. — Had meeting with Mr Spooner and arranged with him about going on with his inspection — Gave him a Statement shewing where work was to inspect & what he might do each day — Made arrangements with Mr Cameron about emigrants and taking their Stock — With Mr Ritchie about various matters —

Wednesday 30 April

Went to Castle at 5 A.M. got keys of wine cellar etc from Sir James breakfasted there & left by the Steamer with Sir James & Lady Matheson, Capt & Mrs Burnaby etc at 1/2 past 6 A.M. — had a pleasent passage and nothing occured in the way of business till we got to Oban at 1/2 past 9 P.M. when and where McNab came on board with an Edin^h agent and an Officer at Arms to serve a Summons on Sir James — Mr Munro wished to see Sir James and wrote him a letter, but Sir James made no reply & did not see him as he could say nothing till he saw his agents in Edin^h — Sir James heard from Mr Callander on the same subject. Left Oban at 10 P.M.

Friday 16 May

On board the Marquis of Laff[?]
in the Sound of Barnera —
Greater part of the Emigran[ts]
the upper part of [illegible] have [brought]
their luggage — Sent John [the]
ground officer over the Carlo[way]
district to tell the Emigran[ts]
that [are] to be on board
their luggage tomorrow; and
North of Galson to be at
Port of Ness all ready to co[me on]
board at 3 A.M. Tuesda[y]
Sent notice to [Tolsta] that [the]
Steamer will call off that pl[ace]
early on Tuesday and th[ey]
to be all ready — Wrote to [them]
for various articles requir[ed by]
Emigrants — Landed on Lit[tle]
and walked over that Isla[nd]
[illegible]

Thursday 1 May

The weather still continues fine and we are making a fine passage — Arrived at Greenock at 1/2 past 11 A.M. Sir James & party proceeded to Glasgow by Steamer, I remained at Greenock. Called on Mr Thomson of the Greenock Bank who is agent for the Duke of Argyll, and who sent several cargoes of Emigrants from this port of the Dukes people as well as some from Perth shire. Asked him various questions regarding Emigration but got no new information from him but that the Dukes people who were sent last year, were doing well & anxious that their friends should follow them — He could tell me of no vessels ready to charter. Left Greenock at 1/2 past 12 and got to Glasgow at 1.15 proceeded direct to Messrs I Ewing & Co^y to see Mr Davidson, found that he had arranged for the Duntroon Castle to go to Stornoway in place of the "Mary Jane" till the "Islay" was ready, that Mr Morison had thrown up the agency of the Steamers, and refused to act or give the necessary information. Was disappointed to find that no Emigrant ship had been chartered except the "Barlow" and that there was no certainty when even that vessel would be ready — Went with Mr Davidson to call on several Ship Agents — Called on Mr McArthur but did not find him in his office — accompanied Mr Auld of Auld & Colvile to the Broomielaw and inspected the ship "Wolfville" offered for Emigrants, did not find the Captn on board & could not ascertain whether he would go to Loch Roag, Appointed to meet in the course of an hour — Went to the "Mary Jane" to look for Mr McArthur and gave Captn Hudson directions how to act and not to deliver the ship without a letter from Mr Davidson — Sent Captn Hudson to examine the Wolfville who reported favoura[b]ly of her — Left a message for Mr McArthur to meet me at the Exchange at 5 P.M. Met the Master of the Wolfville and did all I could to induce him to go to Loch Roag but to no purpose, he offers to go from Clyde @ £3.5/- per full Statute passenger, but I could not engage him as he would not agree to go to Loch Roag, or get another ship to sail along with him. If we have to send the Steamer she will take the cargoes of two ships to Clyde. Went to the Exchange but did not meet Mr McArthur — Accompanied Captn Burnaby to shop — Dined with Sir James & Lady Matheson had meeting afterwards with Mr McArthur and ta[l]ked over the proposed arrangements for running the "Islay" Steamer to Stornoway — Fixed on a meeting for tomorrow at 11 A. M. with Mr McEwan & him to arrange further about the Steamers sailings

Friday 2 May

Went to the "Mary Jane" Steamer to consult Captn about expence of going to Loch Roag and arranged various matters with the Captn — Called at the Wolfville but did not find the master on board, returned to the hotel to breakfast. Called on Mr Davidson & asked him to come to meet Mr McEwan who called at the hotel where we went over a Contract which the Owners of the "Islay" are asked to sign, Sir James making several modifications as it was read over, and to which Mr McEwan agreed so far as he was concerned & he thought his co-owners would at once agree to these conditions — Arranged with Mr McBride of Messrs Hutchinsons & Co^y to ferry Scotts sheep & gave him Memorandum of Place & day of call — Went to Broomielaw to see the Captn of the Duntroon Castle and explained to him when & where he was to find the sheep to be certain that there will be no misunderstanding, also told him of Scaliscro sheep which he would find at Balmacara. Wrote letters to Mr Cameron to have emigrants ready at Loch Roag on 12 & 13 Cur^t where the Steamer would call for 500 — Wrote Mr Gair etc etc — Called on Messrs Reid & Murray and asked them if they could contract for sending 500 Emigrants to Quebec, they said they had no ships & could get no ships at present in Clyde but that they would go to Liverpool to look out for ships on our account, I wished them to write to their agent there before going & that I would wait their answer — Proceeded to Edin^h by the 4 P.M. train with Sir James & Lady Matheson — met Mr Callender & Mr Rhind about McNabs a/c and had some conversation on that subject in presence of Sir James. Arranged to meet next day — Went to look for Howitt but could not make out his lodgings — Saw him in the course of the evening —

Saturday 3 May

Breakfasted with Sir James & Lady Matheson and saw them off to London by the North British Railway — Went to Mr Callenders office and remained there the greater part of the day going over last years a/cs — Consulting about McNabs a/c and giving Mr C. all the particulars regarding it — Had a meeting with Mr Alex. Gair about his accounts   Mr C agreed to pay him a sum to a/c in the mean time — Wrote letters to various parties in Glasgow fixing meetings for Monday —

Monday 5 May

Left Edin^h by the 7.30 A.M. train Called on Messrs Auld & Colvile to ascertain if they had secured a second vessel to go with the Wolfville to which they answered that they had several in view, and asked me to accompany Mr Auld to the Broomielaw to see the ships — Spent the greater part of the day among the Shipping but did not succeed in getting a second ship, and as I saw I was losing time in looking for vessels here without success, called on Reid & Murray and after several proposals from them arranged that Mr Reid should proceed this evening to Liverpool to secure ships to carry 500 passengers @ £3.5/- per head, that he will write me immediately on his getting ships fixing the time & place of meeting — Went to Wishaw by the 5 P.M. train to see my friends there

Tuesday 6 May

Left Wishaw by the 10 A.M. train   Met Messrs McEwan, Ramsay and McArthur and went over Contract for working the Stornoway Steamer trade to which they were willing to agree but could not sign the Contract till hearing from or seeing the rest of the Owners, they wished the time limited to two years & the penalty to £500, agreed to the first but not to the second proposal — Arranged to meet again tomorrow evening to arrange finally when they expect to hear from Mr Brown of Edinburgh. Called for and afterwards dined with Mr Baird of the Dest. Com^{ee} and had conversation with him on various subjects connected with the Highlands. He said we might go on expending the money they had set apart for the Lews — Called on several parties. Wrote letters to Sir James, Mr Callander etc etc Revised answers to McNabs summons & returned same to Edin^h —

Wednesday 7

Made various calls during the forenoon. Went to Reid & Murrays & heard that Mr R had engaged one vessel to carry 300 passengers & that he was looking out for another — Saw Captn Hudson and told him to engage a crew & get coals into the "Marquis" to be ready to sail for Loch Roag on Friday — Arranged with Mr McArthur that he & Captn Hudson were to value the stages planks etc on the Quay belonging to the "Mary Jane" and also to value the articles in that Steamer belonging to the "Marquis", that we were to get these things in exchange for the planks and McArthur was to pay whatever the valuation was more than the value of the planks. He is entitled to all the furnishings found on the Mary Jane as he bough[t] her as she stood with all the furnishings then on board — Had a meeting with Messrs McEwan & Ramsay regarding the Stornoway trade, when they shewed me their correspondence with Mr Brown of Edin^h recommending him to join them in entering into the proposed Contract, which he declined, and on that account they stated their inability to sign it, but at same time stated their determination to carry out every part of it —I tried them in every possible way by threats and arguments but could not get them to enter into the Contract tho' they said they were in honor bound to carry it out — I wished them to give me a letter stating their views & expressing in writing their willingness to act properly in regard to the trade, with a copy of their correspondence with Mr Brown which they promised to do by tomorrow, which letters I would forward to Sir James for his consideration, leaving it to him to say if he was satisfied or if he would resume the trade with the "Marquis" — Went to Wishaw with the 9 o'clock mail train — Wrote Sir James —

Thursday 8

Met with Messrs McEwan & Ramsay and got a letter from them promising to carry on the Stornoway trade with copy of their correspondence with Mr Brown — Arranged sailing days and other arrangements to be gone into if Sir James agrees to allowing them to enter on the trade without a Contract — Had a call from a Mr D. Ross reporter for the Inverness Advertiser saying he intended to go to Stornoway, told him I would be glad to see him there, he seemed favourably inclined — Purchased bread & meal for Emigrants, called on Contractors for tin ware & bedding & told them to have all on board the Steamer tomorrow morning — Called at Nisbits & purchased 4 sets of beam scale and weights to send with Emigrants. Called on Cross & Son about guano & bone dust to be sent to Lews — Called at Reid & Murrays to contract for sending the Emigrants up the Country on their arrival at Quebec but as Mr Reid has not returned who knows these rates, put off till tomorrow — Met Mr Wilson by accident in Nisbits shop but harldy [*sic*] exchanged words — Spent the evening with Mr Davidson & McArthur arranging various matters

Friday 9

Wrote letters to various parties and prepared for leaving Glasgow. Called on Messrs Reid & Murray and got our agreement extended in proper shape & fixed to have the Emigrants at Troon to be put on board their vessels on the 20th or 21st but the vessels to wait till the 28 free of charge — Called on Mr Davidson & went with them to the owners of the "Barlow" to ask if she had left Sunderland, and when might she be expected at Loch Roag — Waited nearly two hours for Mr Callander who intended to accompany me — Having got my business completed so far as practicable, left Glasgow at 12.40 P.M. but the Engineer not having got the Engine to work at first, did not get to Greenock till 3.20 P.M. which we past without calling — The evening was very fine and we had a good passage so far, the vessel sailing 13 to 14 knots

Saturday 10

Past Scaravore Light House at 4 A.M. Barra Head at 8 A.M. and arrived in the Sound of Barnera after a pleasant passage at 5.30 P.M. 26 1/4 hours from Greenock a distance of 330 miles — Mr John McDonald and Mr Cameron came out to meet us and piloted the Steamer into harbour — After making arrangements for shipping Emigrants started by boat with the Captⁿ and Mr Cameron to Callanish having a head wind and tide took nearly three hours to get up — Met Mr Munro & Mr Morison at Callanish received my letters there — proceeded to Stornoway and arrived there at 1 A.M. Sunday morning —

Monday 12 May

At office meeting during the whole day examining what had been doing in my absence, Meeting Mr Munro on various subjects, Mr Wm Morison regarding his accounts, explained to him what is thought of his conduct in throwing up the agency in such an irregular manner, he denies that he refused to give any information he was in possession of, on the contrary he says he offered it — He also states that he can produce a note from Sir James authorising him to advertise for May — Wrote dispatches for the Steamer — Arranged with Mr Cameron to start for Loch Roag tomorrow to superintend the shipping of the Emigrants — The "Duntroon Castle" arrived from Loch Inver at 7 P.M. which we past at Greenock on Friday last   Mr Scobie arrived by her — Saw the Captn of the "Duntroon" and questioned him about his not calling for Scotts sheep, He says Scotts man met him at Portree and told him if he could not take on board the whole of the sheep he need not go for any of them and that he would rather get them across with small boats than divide the lot — Received offers for stable at Loch Morskill but so high that I could not think of accepting them —

Tuesday 13 May

Writing letters for Steamer — Had conversation with Mr Scobie regarding McNabs a/c — McNab having written him on the subject to which he answered rather unguardedly — his memory seems to have failed him about Binnies appointment.   I fear McNab may found on Mr S's letter — Requested him to send a copy of it to Mr Callander — Had also some talk with him about the terms of Captn Hudsons engagement, he says Mr Matheson of Glasgow agreed to give him £50 a year of a bonus besides his pay, as the Steamers were not paying I did not pay the bonus for the last two years which the Captn now claims — As Mr Scobie stated that Captn Hudson was to be paid at the same rate as the Captn of the Portree Steamer, went to Captn McDonald and asked him the terms of his engagement which are £3 per week and a bonus of £30 per annum if all goes right — Attended a Justice of Peace Court (the Sheriff was the only other Justice present) for licensing public Houses — Renewed the certificates of all the old houses but granted no new ones — Laid down certain regulations to be observed by publicans vizt, that they were not to have their shops open after 8 P.M. and that they were not to be allowed to sell spirits in back shops or allow people to sit and tipple in such back shops — which regulation if carried out will be production of much good, and it is hoped reduce the consumption of spirits — Returned to the office & was engaged meeting Emigrants and giving them information on various subjects & appointing with them where & when to embark — going over various a/cs and writing letters —

Wednesday 14

At office arranging with various emigrants — Writing letters to Rev^d Mr McGrigor & Mr McRae Ness etc etc. Meeting several parties — Went to call on Mr Munro & there met the Rev^d Mr McRae, went over what had been done in the Stornoway Glebe case — Mr McRae and the Presbytery have entirely altered their position, they now say that they have possession of more than the Statute glebe of 8 acres at Tong — That they have made a new discovery, that there is a whole field over and above the 8 acres of Glebe & that they cannot give up their right to this without additional compensation — that the money compensation of £38 is only for pasture — That fuel is more expensive in Stornoway — Peats not being so convenient, also that the cottage wants may privilidges which the Minister enjoys at Tong — I reminded him of our arrangement, that he was to get the cottage with some additions in exchange for the Manse of Tong, that he was to get 8 acres of glebe with suitable offices for his glebe at Tong and £38 for the pasture or difference of value to which he then agreed and seemed much satisfied and thanked me most cordially for bringing about such an unexpected arrangement — I then told him that I was ready & authorised by Sir James to carry out & conclude the agreement in every respect as at first contemplated but that there my powers stopt, and that I would not recommend Sir James to go farther in the matter — To which Mr McRae replied significantly that the Presbytery would not let him off so easily — Attended a meeting of the Poor Law Board called specially to reconsider the minute of 18 April last, the members of the Board except Mr Munro & myself were for withdrawing the power from the Inspector of supporting the able bodied and depriving him of the extra pay promised at that meeting — Mr Ross has already acted for one month on the instructions of the Board and expended only about £2, while £12 was paid by Mr Leitch last year during the same period to poor not on the Roll — Mr Ross stated that he held the Board liable for the additional salary & that it could not recal[*l*] its former arrangements — After discussing the question for four hours Mr Wm Munro carried a motion cancelling the minute of 18 April — and Alex^r Morison tho' he & his party voted for Mr Munros motion moved a counter motion after seeing their mistake which was also carried & left matters as they found them — Went to office to write letters, meet Emigrants etc etc.

Thursday 15 May

Went to office and was engaged meeting & paying Ministers Stipends & School Masters salaries — The Rev^d Mr Watson produced a most extraordinary a/c of £31 made up of various idal claims for damages for manse not being repaired, damages to pasture etc etc which I denied & refused payment in toto and stated to Mr Watson my surprize at his presenting such an a/c — He replied that he would not have done so but that he was hard pressed for cash, having to pay the whole of his stipend for his stock, I offered to give him some delay in the payment of £20 to £30 if he withdrew the a/c which he refused but wished to refer it which I refused as I considered the whole to be absurd — Wrote letters for Packet, gave Mr Ritchie instructions on various subjects also to Mr Morison — Left at 1/2 past 2 P.M. for Callanish where I met Mr John Morison Sn[r] attempting to collect his debts from the Emigrants but with little success — Called at Linshader & proceeded to the Sound of Barnera, arrived on board the Steamer at 10 P.M. Met Mr Cameron there — only two families had shipped their luggage —

Friday 16 May

On board the Marquis of S[t]afford in the Sound of Barnera — The greater part of the Emigrants in the upper part of Uig have shipped their luggage — Sent John M[c]kenzie ground officer over the Carloway district to tell the Emigrants from that quarter to be on board with their luggage tomorrow, and all north of Galson to be at the Port of Ness all ready to come on board at 3 A.M. Tuesday mor[nin]g. Sent notice to Tolsta that the Steamer will call off that place early on Tuesday and the emigrants to be all ready — Wrote to Stornoway for various articles required for Emigrants — Landed on Little Barnera and walked over that Island the weather being very fine & most favourable for our purpose — Landed Tin ware & bedding for the Barlow & put them under J M[c]Donald charge.

Saturday 17 May

The passengers are still coming very slowly on board with their luggage, sent John M[c]Donald to Tolsta Cailish & Carloway to push them off with their luggage — Wrote full instructions for Mr Cameron for his guidance in treating with Messrs Leid & Murray for forwarding the Emigrants from Quebec up the Country — Gave him my agreement with Mess[rs] Leid & Murray and all the information I am in possession of — wrote letters to various parties — Gave instructions to the mate to allow no more luggage to come on board as all the remaining room will be required for the Emigrants at Ness & Tolsta — The Capt[n] and Mr Munro arrived from Stornoway at 7 P.M. — Left the Steamer for Stornoway at that hour & got there at one A.M.

Monday 19

Left home accompanied by Mr Cameron at 6.30 A.M. for Callanish breakfasted there and took boat for the Sound of Barnera, having a gale of wind ahead & a heavy sea, did not get to the Steamer till 2 P.M. Mr Murray of Leid & Murray with his brother arrived at the Steamer soon after, Also D[r]

Millar & the Rev^d Mr Campbell. The Emigrants having come on board an allowance of buscuit equal to one pound per adult passenger was served out, with tinware to each passenger who had money to pay for it — After this was done the Rev^d Mr Campbell gave the Emigrants a suitable address with prayer & praise — Had to refuse the greater number of the Emigrants from Barnera to keep room for those at Ness and Tolsta — Having got all on board who had sent their luggage last week sailed from the Sound of Barnera at 12 P.M. — with 400 emigrants on board

Tuesday 20

Arrived at the Port of Ness at 3 A.M. having had rather a disagreeable passage from Loch Roag there being a heavy swell, which brough[t] on Sea Sickness among the women & children and the appearance in the morning of the decks & fore hold were anything but agreeable — Landed at Port immediately on arrival and walked about for some time before any of the Emigrants appeared — Had considerable difficulty in getting the fishermen to get out their boats to put the Emigrants on board the Steamer, but after losing much time & using entreaty & force by turns got the Emigrants with their luggage all in boats, but observed the first boat sent to the Steamer returning with her cargo without getting it on board — On proceeding on board the Steamer found that the Uig people had rebelled against allowing any of the Ness people on board saying that there were quite enough on board — That there being feaver and Small pox at Ness they would not allow a man on board at this place — I remonstrated with them but to no effect, and the Ness men having taken fright returned to the Shore — Seeing that no good could be done here, ordered the Captn to proceed on his voyage — After we left the port of Ness, called the leading men among the Emigrants one by one & explained to them their position — Told them that if we had not the full compliment for the two ships, they would be detained at Troon till the Steamer could return from Lews with another cargo, and that if they did not object we would call at Tolsta and take on board the Emigrants there, which was done without the least trouble, making up the number on board to 450 full Statute Passengers — After leaving Tolsta went to the Captn & told him that I did not wish to come to an anchor in Stornoway Harbour but if he did it must be far out for a short time — The Captn replied that he had to take his family on board & that it would not answer to put his wife & children into a small boat, but I did not think he would persevere in this opinion till on nearing the harbour of Stornoway Mr Munro came to me and said I should go to speak to the Captn for he was determined to go direct to the Quay — I immediately went to the Bridge and told him I wanted the Steamer to come to anchor at Gloomaig Bay, which he refused to comply with saying that he would go direct to the Quay and land every passenger in order to get the vessel cleaned. — I tried to shew him the danger of this as we could not get them all on board again, besides that there was no necessity for it, as he could clean one end of the vessel by moving the Emigrants to the other and vizi versa — But in answer to this I got nothing but an out & out refusal coupled with much insolent talk. I repeated my request in presence of witnesses but met with the same answer saying that I was under his control as well as all on board and that he would do as he pleased — That he was responsible for the lives of all on board and that he would not go to sea till he had landed every passenger washed & fumigated the vessel which would take till next morning — I admitted that he was responsible for the passengers that if he insisted on landing then he might land them on Arnish till he had washed out the vessel, but that I saw no difficulty in doing all the washing required without any of the passengers landing — Notwithstanding all my entreaties he proceeded into the harbour & was making for the Quay till prevented by the number of fishing boats at anchor between him & the Quay — Immediately on letting go the anchor at one P.M. he proceeded on shore, remained there for a considerable time, and was engaged thereafter with all the sea men till 6 P.M. taking on board his furniture & family, never having looked after the passengers, the cleaning of the ship which he thought so important, and prevented the men from doing so having them all employed at his domestic arrangements — Thus detaining nearly 500 Emigrants for 5 hours under heavy rain. I was during this time on board writing letters to Sir James, Mr Davidson etc etc & making several arrangements with the Emigrants — Sent for the D^{rs} & had them all inspected of whom they reported favourably — Landed from the Steamer at 6 P.M. when she sailed — but the Engineer not understanding the Engine allowed the Condensers to get hot, so that at 1/2 past 8 the steamer was not much past Arnish Point, but about that time she got away —

Wednesday 21

Went to the office and was engaged writing letters, meeting parties etc — Arranged finally terms of lease with John Mitchell for part of Scaliscro rent to be £50 per annum while the Uig Road forms the march, but if it is found that he cannot keep that march he is to be deprived of Clettich Oag and the Stream of that name is to form the south boundary the rent to be reduced to £45 — Arranged with John McKay for his taking Soval Cottage for one year at a rent of £9 — the reason for the rent being so low is that he cannot get a lisence till Martin^s — Had a meeting with Mr Ogelvy of Buchen who has come here to purchase cattle — Sent John McDonald with him to Kean Resort to see the Cattle there — The "Islay" arrived, and by her Mr & Mrs Milbank, Mr Ramsay & Mr McArthur — Arranged with the former about conveyances for tomorrow, and was the whole afternoon with the latter arranging about the sailing of the Steamer and calling on parties here — Let the Store & Steamer pier to them for one year @ £40, and arranged for the conveyance of 50 Emigrants to Glasgow @ 5/- per head or Statute passenger — Writing dispatches till 2 A.M.

Thursday 22 May

Went to the Steamer Quay and there mustered the Emigrants, about 70 souls, but making 51 Statute passengers. Had some difficulty in getting them all away, some of their baggage having been arrested — Went to the office & met various parties, arranged to get work for the Emigrants who are waiting the Barlow. Arranged with Mr Ritchie to go to Kean Reasort to see sheep draining doing there & to point out ground to be drained, to Bethune also to clear away in front of cottage etc. Attended meeting of the shareholders of the Water Co^y called to consider the necessity of raising more capital (20/- per share) to pay off the debts of the Company, which was agreed to, Mr J.R. Mackenzie objecting in very strong terms declaring that he would not pay & having lost his motion left the meeting in a high state of exitement — Returned to office & had meeting with Rev^d Mr Leid Lochs about the School of that Parish now vaccant. Mr Dunoon who is recommended by Mr Watson Cromarty & now at Lochs not being approved of by Mr Leid — Mr McRae of Stornoway wishes to get the School for his son — Had a call from the Rev^d Mr McLean late of Back who offers to accompany the Emigrants to America & remain with them for one year on condition that he is paid £150 and gets a free passage for himself & family. I told him that Sir James would pay a cabin passage for himself but I did not think he could be expected to pay the expences of his family which he could defray out of his salary — That perhaps we might get an intermediate birth fitted up for him & his family which would not altogether cost more than £20, but told him I could not give him any decided answer till I had heard from Sir James — Meeting with various parties, who offer security for the payment of their rents etc etc Had a call from Leiut Risk of H.M.S. Tartarus which vessel is here at present looking after the fisheries — Gave him leave to fish.

Friday 23

Great numbers of the Ness Fishermen have come to town and are calling at the office with letters from the Curers becoming bound for the payment of their rents, as I prevented their cutting peats till they had either paid their rents or given satisfactory Security, this rule applies to all who were served with notices of removal over the whole Estate but it will be difficult to carry it out, tho' already many are coming forward to pay or give security — Went to Steamers office to get Inventory made out of things there to be valued over to Owners of "Islay" — Investigated claim made by Kenneth Murray for boxes of eggs said to be lost in Steamer and refused to pay same there being no proper grounds for such claim — Attended sale of Mr James R McIvers furniture — Had meeting with Mr Munro & Mr Thomson the tenant of Holm Curing Station who finds some difficulty in preventing other curers from using the Station and occupying the land let to him for fish curing purposes — Mr Munro thinks he cannot prevent them — He agrees to take his chance if I allow him to exact payment of net ground from the other boats fishing at Holm —

Saturday 24 May

At office writing letters & meeting parties Mr John McLeod, James McDonald, Master of "Union" and J.R. McIver regarding debt against the former which he agrees to leave in Mr McIvers hands for me — meeting various people from the Country who are calling with letters of security for payment of rents to get power to cast their peats — Messrs Ogilvy having returned from Kean Reasort & Reef where they had seen the ca[s]ttle arranged to take them on the following terms 57 at Reef @ 40/- per head and 170 at Kean Reasort @ 35/- each with power to cast 15 out of the latter — Sent a messenger to get the cattle sent over to be delivered. Examining accounts and arranging various matters at the office —

Monday 26 May

At the office all the day writing letters for the packet, going over Kennedy & Co^{ys} account and corrispondence regarding Extra Work at Sandwick Hill which is quite unfounded tho' no doubt they may have been detained a little for want of tiles — Wrote to Sir James on the subject — Settling with servants for Half Years wages etc — Arranged with Mr Ogilvy for ferrying the cattle, the expence of which he is to pay — Am annoyed by several of the Emigrants who are waiting the "Barlow", sent some of them to work at the grounds — & wrote J. McDonald Barnera to set others to work for Destitution meal — Meeting with various parties regarding giving up Houses & others entering, getting rents etc etc

Tuesday 27 May

Went to office and met several of the Country people asking for leave to cut their peats & giving every assurance of paying their arrears of rents at the Market — In many cases got letters of Security from the Fish Curers & Stornoway Merchants & some little cash — Revised conditions of sale for Roup of Cattle in calf & calved purchased from Emigrants, sold about a score at an average of 44/- each — A few were left unsold — Walked over grounds, Castle offices etc — The lime is telling already on the grass, I never saw it looking so green — The grub is very severe on the oats and barley particularly that first sown — Returned to the office and again met several

Country people — McRae Scaliscro regarding the fence to be built for him at Reef, which he refuses to occupy till completed, but satisfied him on this point by arranging to set it agoing without delay — Wrote Uig ground officer, etc etc arranging with parties who bought cattle today —

Wednesday 28 May

Had a lengthened interview with Mr Scott of Park who again offered to give up his farm if his Stock was taken & meliorations paid as at the end of the lease — This he said was altogether on account of his neighbouring with so many small tenants who used liberties with his stock — He considers his farm a very good one and not high rente[n]d if it had better boundaries — which certainly might be improved by removing a few people — Settled with Mr Scott for his wintering — Packet arrived and was much relieved by hearing of the safe arrival of the Emigrants at Troon — Steamer also arrived but had not the pleasure of hearing from Sir James by either opportunity — Meeting with various country people and writing dispatches for Steamer till one A.M. Am much perplexed at hearing that the Barlow is still at Sunderland and no prospect of her sailing

Thursday 29

Went to Mary Bank and there delivered over to Mr Ogilvy 47 three year olds at 40/-, wintered at Reef and 153 young cattle @ 35/- part of which were wintered at Holm and others purchased from Emigrants — Saw the cattle in to the Quay, and settled with Mr Ogilvy who paid £360 — I hope he will find the cattle to answer his purpose and that he will be induced to make another visit. Had meeting with the Banker regarding his sons a/c for Steamers and security for rents of Ness Fishermen — Had meeting with Mr James MacKenzie regarding Free Church Manse & School Charter — Went with Alex^r Forbes to Mr Munros office and took his evedence on J Kennedy & Co^ys claim which is satisfactory — Settled with workmen on Uig road & placed the greater part of their earnings to C^r of rents — Meeting numbers of people from the Country wishing for leave to cut peats etc etc —

Friday 30th May

Arranged with John Mackenzie about Kelp making in the Barvas district, and disposal of cattle still on hand — Went to Sand^k Hill and met the tenants of Melbost. Let to them about 30 acres of Sand^k Hill at 20/- per acre — Proceeded to Garabost and remained there all day paying workmen and taking inventory of tools, iron and other articles at the Tile Work, discharged several of the work people, and gave others notice that their services would not be required after next month. As the drainage works are now about being completed and no demand for bricks or tiles I fear these works must be thrown idle — on account of the great expence of cartage to and from the works & the high price which must be paid for coals, with other causes tiles cannot be made here so cheap as farther south & if they have to be exported there will be an additional charge for freight —

Saturday 31 May

Went to office and examined the pay bills for work at Grounds, Garden Plantations and Home Farm, sent a Clerk to pay the work people & wrote Mr Ritchie to reduce the number of workmen to one half. Had meetings with various parties, Mr J McLeod, Mr Nicolson, Mr J.R. McIver etc — writing letters & meeting with Country people etc etc —

Monday — 23 June

[went] to office and met [Dauns?]
[p]eople from the Country — [Wr]
[a] letter to each of the Ground of[ficers?]
[te]lling them to warn the peo[ple]
[o]f their respective districts
[ca]me to the market with their [cattle?]
— be on the ground early on
[ma]rket day & to take a list of
[p]eople who attend with Sto[ck]
[th]e number & value of such [cattle?]
[a]nd warn them to go to pa[y]
[th]eir rents with the money
[th]ey receive — So that it may
[b]een who sells & does not pa[y]
[re]nt — Settled with the Own[er]
[o]f the "Kudow" and gave h[im]
[a]n order on Mr. R. E. Mathe[son?]
[o]f Glasgow for £ 698..11.5 be[ing]
[th]e balance of freight due [on?]
[wr]ote letters for the Packet

Monday 2nd June

Went to Patent Slip to inspect work done there by James Anderson at Smithy & Stove — Inspected House occupied by Murdo Leid Baker and shop taken by John Campbell both in D^r McIvers old houses which require some repairs — At office writing letters for the Packet, going over Wm Morison & Co^{ys} a/cs for Steamers, which are sent to Mr I.E. Matheson Glasgow for settlement — Went over and examined monthly accounts, and granted orders for payment of same — I am mobbed by people from all quarters who are waiting the "Barlow" and have become almost desparate — Many of them no doubt are very ill off having sold their all, expecting to have got off nearly a month ago — Appointed to meet all who are willing to work tomorrow at Bayhead — Wrote John McDonald Barnera to send the Emigrants left there (& who are entirely destitute) to Stornoway & that they would get work —

Tuesday 3 June

Went to Guirshader accompanied by Mr Houston & laid off work for the Emigrants waiting the Barlow, offered to furnish them with tools and pay them every evening for what they worked, but they all refused to work except two or three who began at once — They said I would be compelled to give them food as the vessel did not come when promised & if they did not get meal they would go & kill & eat the sheep which were purchased from them. I told them they would get no meal but what they worked for, if they took the sheep for which they had been paid I would see them punished — Went to office and wrote several letters. Had meeting with John McDonald & J.R. McIver about settlement of their a/cs — Attended meeting of the Water co^y where it was resolved to make an additional call of 10/- per share payable on the 1st July and another call of 10/- per share payable on the first of August — This money to be applied in paying of the debts of the Co^y — Accompanied Mr J M^{c}kenzie to see drain required at Free Manse — called at the Free School and was much pleased at Mr McMasters method of teaching, the children seem to be making great progress — Returned to office to write letters — Settled with the Back tenants for work done on the Tolsta Road — Met various people from the Country asking for authority to cut peats, but in most cases refused if they did not pay or find Security — Went to Holm to see what Mr D Mackenzie is about, he is now all alone & says he has a good deal to do yet — Asked him to come to town tomorrow to settle a/cs — The crop is all laid down on this farm consisting of Lint (doing very well) Potatoes & Turnip. Had a walk with McIntosh & saw what he was about — Went to the Castle to see work now doing in front of same etc etc —

Wednesday 4 June

Went to the office and met several parties who wish permission to cut peats, Emigrants etc — Arranged several matter[s] with John McDonald the Uig Ground Officer — Wrote letters and arranged several a/cs — Attended meeting of Parochial Board from 12 to 5 called to approve of Assessment Roll, but the time was mostly taken up with trifling discussion. Mr Ross the Inspector by a resollution of the majority of members there present was instructed to stop proceedings against Mr J.R. Mackenzie for his arrears of assessment in 1849, tho' he had got two decisions of the Sheriff against him & repeated instructions from the board on the subject — The Steamer & Packet arrived Was engaged till 12 0'clock writing dispatches for the former — All the bulls on St Columns Island except three being sold, let the same from last term to Mr McDonald Crobeg. The rent to be fixed after a survey of the Island by me & Mr Cameron, not to exceed £27 & not to be less than £22. The three remaining bulls to be taken by Mr McDonald.

Thursday 5 June

Went to Gress and remained there all day attending a sale of Cattle, Horses & Farming Impliments — Purchased one horse & one cow for Holm Farm, 6 or 7 more of the latter are required, but the cattle at the sale having sold above their value did not purchase more.

Friday 6 June

Went to the office and arranged several matters, wrote letters etc — Went to Barvas to attend a poor law meeting accompanied by the Rev^d Mr Shipton — Laid on the assessment for the insuing year at the same rate as last year vizt. 1/8d per pound, one half payable by landlord & one half by the tenant, Met the ground officer at Barvas & gave him instructions about Kelp making — to collect Sheep purchased from Emigrants etc etc Got home at 11 P.M. The weather being exceedingly cold —

Saturday 7 June

At the office all day going over accounts meeting parties, John McRae about fence to be built at Reef, wrote ground officer enclosing offers for the work @ 11d and 1/- per yard directing him to point out the ground to the Contractors — Mr E McIver regarding rent of Gress which he promised to settle for next week — Master of Mr Milbanks yacht and arranged with him to proceed to Loch Seaforth where he could get a settlement from his employer I not being in funds to do so — Went to the Castle and saw Mrs Watson on various matters. Went over grounds and saw what is doing etc —

Monday 9 June

At office meeting parties who have called for leave to cut their peats & pay arrears of rent — Settled with Mr Wm Fairbairn for his accounts during Mr Scobie's & my management, got a discharge in full from him, and gave him his discharge having no further use for his services — Settled with Peter McFarlane for his a/cs during Mr Scobies management, & after much difficulty & loss of time got him to sign a discharge in full — Had a meeting with John Fraser Baker and arranged his a/c for same period but refused to pay him as he would not allow me to retain payment of his feu duty — His objection to not paying is that he wants 10 feet of the frontage stated in his charter which has evidently been a mistake in making out the deed — Called on Mr Munro to take his advice on the subject — which he is to consider for a day or two — My idea is to prosicute for payment of the feu duty and make the party who made the mistake liable — The ground on both sides being now built upon none can be added — Mrs Morison on the north side of Frasers feu occupies 2 feet 4 Ins more than her ground, and there is a passage between both feus of 5 feet which if added to the latter would make the difference of 5 feet — Mrs Morison's is an old charter & the ground built upon 80 years ago

Tuesday 10 June

Went to the office and gave audiance to numbers of people from the Country about payment of rents, peat cutting, Emigration etc — Wrote several letters, made an agreement with Donald McDonald, BlackSmith to do all the smith work on the proprietors farms at the rate of 50/- per annum for each pair of Horses — Was engaged the whole remaining part of the day with Mr J.R. McIver settling Mr Scobie's a/cs which are at last finally arranged with him. Also all a/cs with the proprietor to this date — Went to the Castle and went over the whole building with Mr Howitt & Mrs Watson to see the things ordered to be done by Lady Matheson and arranged that they should be gone on with at once — Went to Gress to see about some sheep draining wanted to be done by Mr E McIver Arranged with Hector Calder to do same @ one penny per rood for single drains, and two pence for double drains — Remained at Gress for the night —

Wednesday 11 June

Arranged regarding some repairs required to be done on buildings at Gress by tenant under old lease before they can be taken off his hands — Arranged for payment of Rents now due — Had meeting with tenants of Back, and arranged for their remaining in their present possessions till Martinmas —

Returned to Stornoway — Steamer arrived & also the packet — received a number of letters — Revised Drft Feu Charter for Light House ground — Last months Cash a/c and was detained writing letters at office till 4 A.M. —

Thursday 12 June

Went to office and settled with several Contractors for work done — Wrote letters — Had a meeting with Mr Scott the Contractor for the Light House buildings who is about to start operations. Saw various people from the Country on different subjects — Went to Soval to attend a meeting of the Parochial Board of Lochs — The Inspector has been relieving great numbers in the Carloway district of the able bodied — and had numbers of applications from all parts of the Parish but put them all off till this day fortnight to which day the Board adjourn, and sent notice to all the Constables of the Parish to attend to give evidence of the state of the applicants from each township — After the meeting went over the Luerbost Road and proceeded to Crosbost to point out the site of a Store House to be built by Mr Murdo McLeod. Got home at one A.M. —

Friday 13 June

Went to the office and met the Captn of the "Barlow" who had arrived late last night from Loch Roag — Went to the Custom House with him to arrange for an officer to go over to Loch Roag to inspect the Emigrants etc — Found that the Captain had brought no "Contract tickets" one of which must be given to each emigrant before the vessel can be cleared out — He says it is the duty of the charterers to give these, while I maintained was the duty of the owners of the ship in return for the passage money — As no printed tickets could be had here I asked the Custom House Authorities if they would allow of written tickets being used, but no, they must stand to the Strict letter of the Law & as no time could be lost, and as it would require some smartness to get the tickets back by the first Steamer from Glasgow I determined on sending Mr Morison by boat to the main land, who is to endeavour to work his way the best he can to Glasgow by Monday & return here by the "Islay" on Wednesday, if he can manage this the "Barlow" can be dispatched within her time. Wrote to Glasgow to ascertain who was bound to supply the tickets and bear the expence of sending for them — Arranged with Mr Cameron about shipping the emigrants, he proceeds this evening with the Captn to Loch Roag — At office writing letters and meeting with Country people etc etc —

Saturday 14 June

Went to the office and met various parties from the Country wishing to get power to cut peats some paying small sums of money to a/c of rent, and others presenting letters of security from fish curers etc — Settling accounts with various parties & writing letters. Went to the Castle and inspected alterations making ordered by Lady Matheson, walked over ground with Mr Ritchie, and pointed out several little things to be attended to by Mr Ritchie & Howitt — Returned to office and received letters by packet. Sold 50 quarters of bear to McLennan the Miller @ 27/- per quarter etc etc Went to Melbost in the evening to see Drains for which Mr Houston wants tiles —

Monday 16 June

At office meeting Country people in regard to Emigration, payment of rents etc — Wrote Rev^d Mr McRae Barvas on accounts of Parochial Board etc — Writing letters for the Packet, Settling accounts, met various parties John McDonald, G. officer Uig, Mr Morison, Mr Ross etc —

Tuesday 17 June

At office meeting Country people as to rents, peats etc — Settling a/cs. Going over Poor Law Assessments and writing appeals against various charges, writing letters — Had meeting with Captⁿ of Emigrant Ship and arranged several matters with him

Wednesday 18 June

At office writing letters — Sent Express to Harris to tell Rev^d Mr McLean of the sailing of the "Barlow" and cart for his luggage — Went to the Custom House to arrange for the Comptroller's going to Loch Roag tomorrow to clear out the "Barlow" & Inspect the Emigrants, had to deposit £5 to pay his expenses etc — Sat at Justice of Peace Court when W^o McIver Deanston was tried and fined in the sum of £12.10/- for selling Whisky without a lisence — The Justices recommended that the fine should be lowered to £5 — Attended a meeting of the Parochial Board called to hear Appeals against Assessment and which lasted the greater part of the day — I appealed against the valuation of £270 placed on the Castle Grounds, £40 on the Brick Work £130 on the Patent Slip and several other minor charges, could get no reductions on the grounds, got clear of the ass^t on the Brick Works and a reduction on the Patent Slip etc — Attended an adjourned meeting of Presbytery to consider in regard to the Stornoway Glebe Case. The Rev^d members did not seem to understand one another and had very sharp words — Mr Leid & Mr Watson refusing out & out to agree to the proposed arrangement on the Glebe Case and Mr McRae seeing that he could not make better of it, is disappointed that he cannot get them to sanction even the terms offered, which he cannot blame them for on account of what he himself has said and done — I was asked by the Presbytery if I was prepared to offer more on the part of Sir James to which I answered in the negative, the presbytery then arranged to write Sir James asking if he would offer more — I told them if they did not accept the proposal already made, Mr McRae must just content himself with remaining at Tong — The Steamer arrived & by her Mr Morison with the Emigrant Contract tickets having only left here on Friday evening — The Owner of the Barlow with a surgeon for her also arrived — — Received several papers in McNabs case from Messrs Gordon Stewart & Cheyne, and wrote remarks on same with answers to his charges etc — wrote Mr I E Matheson regarding Morisons a/c etc — Was detained at office till 4 A.M. writing dispatches for the Steamer —

Thursday 19 June

Went to office and arranged various matters — Left for Callanish accompanied by Dr Miller & the Comptroller to see the Barlow off — Attended meeting of Poor Law Board of Uig at Callanish — Proceeded to Tolsta Chailish and went on board the "Barlow" off that place, remained on board till 11 P.M. arranging with passengers, inspecting Stores with Comptroller, berths etc etc The greater number of the passengers are now on board —

Friday 20 June

Went on board the "Barlow" at 10 A.M. and was engaged making up lists of the passengers & Contract tickets — Mustered the whole of the Emigrants and examined them by families & individually in presence of the Custom House & Medical Officers, the owner giving them Contract tickets as they past along — After this was finished the Rev^d Mr Campbell of Uig gave them a long address and baptized a number of children young and old — I thereafter distributed some clothing to the poorest of the Emigrants who were very ill off, being some of what had remained unsold, the Emigrants with the exception of a few families were very respectably clothed and seemed very happy & contented — The Comptroller worked with us all night to get the Ships papers ready for sailing in the morning — He found there was 8 bolls of oat meal short and would not let the vessel sail till this was got fortunately at Callanish — The number on board is 287 souls equal to 221 1/2 Statute passengers —

Saturday 21 June

On board the "Barlow" & having got all ready she weighed anchor at 6 A.M. I took leave of the passengers which was very affecting — They thanked me over & over again & tho' sorry to part seemed pleased with the change they were about to make & with the ship & Captain — The Owner & Captain have really done every thing in their power to accommodate & please — Left the "Barlow" off Carloway where we landed at 7 A.M. We soon lost sight of the ship she having a fair wind & plenty of it — Proceeded to Callanish and having rested & breakfasted left for Stornoway. Called at the Castle & saw what was doing there in my absence — Had meeting with Rev^d Mr McLean who offered to go with the few Emigrants left by the "Barlow" about 30 if Sir James would defray the travelling expenses & passage of himself and family in addition to his salary which I refused to comply with, but offered him £12 in addition to his salary being the rate at which we could have got him out by the "Barlow" had he gone by that vessel which he could have done if he pleased — I do not see what great good he can now do by going as the people will be scattered all over the Canadas by the time he would get out —

Monday 23 June

Went to office and met various people from the Country — Wrote a letter to each of the Ground officers telling them to warn the people of their respective districts to come to the Market with their cattle. The officer to be on the ground early on the Market day & to take a list of the people who attend with Stock, the number & value of such stock, and warn them to go to pay their rents with the money they may receive — So that it may be seen who sells & does not pay the rent — Settled with the Owner of the "Barlow" and gave him an order on Mr I.E. Matheson of Glasgow for £698.11.5 being the balance of freight due him. Wrote letters for the Packet — Had meeting with Mr Gair and Mr Ross about interdicting the Owner or Charterer of the "Glow-Worm" from using the Steamers Quay but consider that this is the business of the tenants of the Quay & I will not interfere in the mean time on the part of the proprietor.

Tuesday 24 June

Walked over Stoneyfield, Holm & Sandwick Hill farms with Mr Ritchie, the Flax Crop at Holm looks very well, also the other crops on that farm & Sand^k Hill. I am sorry there is no prospect of getting any of these farms let — Went to office & met several persons — Attended poor Law Meeting and called on the Sheriff to consult him on matters connected with the Board — Returned to office and arranged with several parties as to payment of rents etc etc —

Wednesday 25

Went to office received letters by Steamer "Islay" at 11A.M. The "Glow-Worm" Chartered by Mr Wm Morison arrived at 6 A.M. — After seeing several parties & arranging various matters proceeded to Lochs to attend a Poor Law meeting accompanied by Mr Peterkin of the board of Supervision where the Constables of all the Townships were present — Went over the Roll of Paupers & also those receiving temporary relief when one third of the number was struck off by the advice of the Constables — Mr Peterkin seemed pleased with this proceeding — Returned to Stornoway and got ready 68 emigrants to sail by the Islay at 4 tomorrow morning equal to 56 Statute passengers, gave some of the most destitute part of the clothes left unsold — Writing dispatches for the Steamer till 12 P.M.

Thursday 26

Called on Mr Ross with Munro the Ness miller to protect him from parties who are threatening him with prosicution on false accounts — Remained at the office all day examining the monthly accounts & granting orders for payment of same, going over rentals & meeting with Country people — Went to Melbost, Goathill etc — Mr Peterkin spent the evening with me & had conversation with him on Poor Law matters —

Friday 27

Went to office and was engaged writing letters & meeting parties till 12 — Went to Poor Law meeting and was detained there till 5 disposing of various cases   Mr Peterkin of the Board of Supervision attended and gave instructions and made various suggestions   Returned to the office & met various parties from the Country regarding payment of rent, leave to cut peats etc — Went to Guirshader & inspected Houses building for poor women & widows, to be removed from Bayhead, two of which are now occupied — Went over ground now being drained by Houston & Co^y — Went to Castle etc

Saturday 28

Went to office & examined plans for repairs of Uig Manse, Plan for improvement of Port of Ness to be sent to Board of Fisheries. Went to Castle and went over building with Mr Howitt — Walked over grounds with Mr Ritchie, fixed on site of cottage for old Murdo & arranged to have it built without delay   Proceeded to Arinish to point out [to] the contractor ground to be taken for Light House — Called for McRae the farmer in order that he might point out some ground he wanted to be sheep drained but found he had left by last Steamer —

Monday 30th June

Had meeting with Mr Kenneth Morison of London about his pier, he intends to extend the breast work in front of his property on the South Beach — Meeting various parties at the office, Mr Cameron about Reef fence, cattle to be sold at the Market etc — Sketched plan for Pipers House at Loch Roag head — revised Specification of repairs of Uig Manse, wrote letters for Packet   Arranged with Bowie for Market dinner etc etc

Saturday 12 July

to Carloway and met the peop[le]
I not see yesterday, took all [?]
I get in ~~Coows~~ Cash and Cattle, th[e]
[catt]le is very scarce at present, a[s]
[p]eople do not wish to part wi[th]
Cattle that have milk, as th[at]
i[s] all they can get in the shape [of ?]
— Proceeded to Callanish & th[e]
[?] the people of that townsh[ip]
is isolated — got in all to da[y]
[to] day 38 head of Cattle & £ 31 [?]
— Returned to Stornoway and [arriv]-
-e at 9 PM —

Monday 14 July

to the office and met various pa[rties]
[wro]te letters — Called on Mr Callen[der ?]
doing McNees business he & [us ?]
having arrived by last Steam[er]
[wen]t to Castle and inspected w[?]

Tuesday 1 July

At office granting orders for meal to Kelp makers — meeting parties about settlement of rents — Writing ground officers not to push the people to make Kelp as the price has fallen — Examining monthly accounts — Meeting Rev^d Mr McRae , Mr Peterkin, Mr Morison — Went to Garabost Brickwork to see what was doing — Told the foreman to give notice to the workmen that they were to be discharged on Saturday week as the work was then to Stop — Returned to the office & met various parties the Inspector of Poor of Barvas, Rev^d Mr Leid Lochs etc Went to the Castle to see Mrs Watson about preparing Market dinner as the Hotel Keepers would not undertake to contract for it — She is to have all ready tomorrow at a cheaper rate and better than if furnished by a Contractor — Walked over part grounds to see what men are doing — Inspected what is doing about Castle etc — John McKay refused to go to the Store to see two stones of meal weighed out — There being little meal on hand & having to give out but very small quantities now and then, I discharged the Storekeeper and send one of the clerks to see the meal weighed out. McKay thought this duty beneath him which would not occupy half an hour per week and refused out & out to obey, for which cause I told him to leave the office as if he did not obey he would be shewing a bad example to others — Saw his brother William & told him that if his brother felt sorry for his conduct & promised to behave better in future I would allow him to come back — Steamer "Islay" arrived & by her Mr Callender etc

Wednesday 2 July

Wrote letters for the Steamer, met various parties — Went to the Market and remained there till 9 P.M. — A number of dealers attended but the prices continue very low. No improvement from last year, but less if anything — There was a good show of Cattle & Horses — Stock seemed in good condition —

Thursday 3 July

Meeting various parties at office — called on Mr Callander and went over unsettled accounts during Mr Scobie's management with him and D Mackenzie. Went to the Market with a clerk to collect rents, got upwards of £100 in small sums, purchased 36 head of Cattle those left unsold at the Market and sold them to John Robertson @ 20/- each. Meeting various parties at the office during the evening settling rents etc —

Friday 4 July

At office meeting country people & receiving rents — Settling with people who sold Cattle to K Morison I having taken J.R. McIver & John McRae as his security & gave the people C^r in their rents for the amount as Morison could not pay for the Cattle — Wrote G Officers not to push the manufacture of Kelp as the price had fallen — Agreed with Angus McLean for the building of the pipers cottage at £5 per rood being £25 for the mason work — Went to Castle and arranged with Mr Howitt about fitting up the old laundry for a Dairy & Milking House. Went over gardin grounds etc

Saturday 5

At office writing letters, arranging various matters with Ground officers Called on Mr Callender with McRae Arinish regarding a/c against him for balance of Stock amounting to £110 — He claims damages for want of wintering the first year of his lease — Mr Scobie is written to on the subject — Arranged with the Ground Officers to meet the tenants of the four parishes at various places & days during the insuing fortnight to collect rents and take Cattle — Settling various a/cs etc

Monday 7 July

Went to office and met various parties from the Country — vizt John McRae Scaliscro, James Mackenzie Erdroal etc — Called on Mr Callender & had conversation on various subjects — Settled with Mr John McAulay Sn^r for accounts during Mr Scobie's management who got a balance of £51.6.4 Wrote letters for Packet — Examined James Andersons a/c for repairs of Laxdale Cottage — Called on Mrs Watt and got payment of House rent under deduction of 17/- laid out by her for repairs etc — Had meeting with Mr Howitt, Mr Ross etc

Tuesday 8 July

Called on Mr Callender and went over papers regarding McNabs a/cs — wrote several letters & meet parties — Went to Coll where I had appointed to meet the people of the District from Tong to Tolsta to pay rents, received only £[*no sum shown*] and 29 cattle tho' I went [*to*] all the people of that district —

Wednesday 9

Went to the office and received Steamer letters — Was engaged the greater part of the day with Messrs Callender Munro & Gair as to dispute regarding the Steamer Quay the "Glow Worm" having come alongside the "Islay" and was landing her cargo over that vessel to the Quay — Mr Gair however kept the gates shut and prevented the goods from being removed, wrote the agent for the other vessel that if he agreed to pay 20/- as Quay dues for this trip and promised not to persist in coming to the Wharf let to the "Islay" Co^y he would let the cargo be landed for this trip, but if not that the "Glow Worm" must at once remove which she did by going to the Public Quay — Writing letters for Steamer to Sir James, Mr I.E. Matheson, Mr Souter etc — Going over accounts for work done by Shedden with Alex^r Mackenzie etc —

Thursday 10 July

Went to the Head of Little Loch Roag to meet the people of Uig with Cattle or Cash to pay their rents, tho' all the tenants west of that point were warned to meet me there few or none appeared, and I did not receive more than £9.12/- in cash and 17 head of cattle — Inspected the Uig Road to Loch Roag not yet quite completed — Also walked over the branch Road to Loch Morskill now about finished — Marked off site of cottage for piper at Loch Roag Head at which several people are employed — Had meeting with McRae the out going tenant of Scaliscro & Mitchell the in coming tenant, regarding dispute between them, McRae having refused to clear the farm of his Stock on the term day, and is still keeping them on, on the plea that he cannot send his stock to Reef till the fencing at that farm is completed — Agreed to refer the matter in dispute to Mr Murdo McAulay on the part of the proprietor, Christopher McRae Mealista for John McRae & Peter Smith Earshader for John Mitchell — The three together to judge what deduction in Mitchells rent should be allowed for the Stock remaining on the farm after the term, and the two former arbiters to say whether such deduction should be given by the proprietor in whole or in part, or if it should be paid by John McRae in the Shape of damage in whole or in part — Returned to Callanish and remained there for the night — I was accompanied today by Mr Callender —

Friday 11 July

Started for Carloway and met people there with Cattle & Cash to pay rents — Proceeded to Barvas & attended a Poor Law Meeting, the Roll was revised & a constable from each township in the Parish being present several were struck off, some of whom I fear ought to have been continued, but the constables of one farm would not hear of the parish being burdened by the poor of another farm — After the meeting returned to Dalbeg & arrived there at 11 P.M. —

Saturday 12 July

Went to Carloway and met the people I did not see yesterday, took all I could get in Cash & Cattle, the former is very scarce at present, and the people do not wish to part with any Cattle that have milk, as they require all they can get in the shape of food — Proceeded to Callanish & there met the people of that township & Braiscalate — got in all today & yesterday 38 head of Cattle & £31/- cash — Returned to Stornoway and got home at 9 P.M. —

Monday 14 July

Went to the office and met various parties   Wrote letters — Called on Mr Callender regarding McNees business he & Mr Knox having arrived by last Steamer   Went to Castle and inspected what was doing in and around the building & gave directions on various matters — Went to Soval to meet the people of Lochs for payment of rents, numbers of them are now absent at the Caithness fishing — Received £55.14/- in Cash and 13 head of Cattle — Proceeded to Callanish and got there at 11 P.M.

Tuesday 15 July

Went to Shawbost and there met the people of both Shawbosts, Bragars & Arnold, but as numbers did not appear with either Cattle or Cash, sent a list to each township of those tenants I wished to see and what Cattle they were expected to bring, fixed to meet them again tomorrow at Arnold River. Returned to Dalbeg and there examined Paybills for Workmen at Grounds, Home, Sand^k Hill & Holm farms, and wrote Mr A McIver with instructions to pay them, retaining as much as possible for arrears of rent. Also wrote to each foreman to reduce the expence to the lowest posssible limit & that if they did not attend to this warning it might be the last — Went over various accounts for Works with Mr McDonald Ness etc —

Wednesday 16 July

Went to Shawbost and inspected the work done at the Quay — this work has not been going on for some time back, but arranged with John Weir that he should commence operations again on Monday first, the workmen to be paid one half with Destitution meal and the other half of their wages to go to C^r of rents — Proceeded to Arnold River and there met numbers of people with Cattle, having purchased them went on to Barvas and took Cattle from the people of that place & Brue. Got today & yesterday 80 head of Cattle and £30/-3/- cash — Proceeded to Swanabost and arrived there at 10 P.M. — Left notice at Barvas for those who did not meet me today to meet on Saturday

Thursday 17

Walked over the Part of the Tolsta & Ness Road as far as Skigersta and let various proportions of it to be paid for, partly in Destⁿ meal and the balance put to C^r of their rents — Returned to Dell River where I had appointed to meet the people of the Ness district with Cattle or Cash to pay their rents, but as few appeared, took notes of the stock possessed by each tenant and sent lists to all the townships stating what Cattle or Horses were required & to meet me tomorrow at Galson — Went on to Galson & arrived there at 11 P.M.

Friday 18 July

Met numbers of the Ness people with Cattle — Sent lists to N Galson, the Borves & Shaders of the Cattle they were expected to bring to meet me at Borve River — Went there and took with those delivered yesterday 70 head of Cattle and £95.15/- cash — Settled with people for Work done at Shader and returned to Galson at 8 P.M.

Saturday 19 July

Went on to Barvas after Settling with work people at Galson, and took Cattle from the Barvas & Galson people and £61.2/- Cash – Called at the manse of Barvas and signed joint minute with Mr McRae appointing Mr Bennitt to the Parish School — Counted over the whole of the Cattle taken on the west side being 234 Cows & 30 Horses and sent them to the neighbourhood of Stornoway — Got home at 9 P.M.

Monday 21 July

At office, reading over letters arrived in my absence — Called on Mr Callender & consulted him as to paying Binnies a/c, arranged to pay him at the rate of one per cent on the Amount Estimated that the Castle Works would come to — Had meeting with Mr Munro & Mr Callender regarding Urquharts claim Also about Kennedy & Co^y — Consigned in Bank the amount admitted to be due the latter party — Writing letters for Packet — Went to Castle & arranged various matters with Mrs Watson. Went to Mary Bank to sort Cattle to be sent to Southill but night came on before I could get this done

Tuesday 22

Went to Mary Bank at 7 A.M. and arranged the Cattle & Horses taken from tenants last week as follows, 80 greys & 7 Horses for Southill 71 cows 40 greys & 21 Horses for Falkirk 35 small animals to be sent to Kean Reasort — 7 Greys & 1 mare & foal to Holm — one Pony for Lady Matheson + 1 cow sold in all 264 — Had meeting with the Rev^d Mr Watson Uig who objects to paying rent, saying that he did not get possession of his farm, Mitchell & his sub tenants not having been removed — These parties got notice of removal but were allowed to remain Mr Watson having arranged with them, and even took rent — Mr Watson offers to pay his rent & admit that he got possession if I agree to give him what he calls good marches, I refused to make any conditions with him till he paid his rent, and threatened to sequestrate if he did not pay at once — Attended meeting of Water Co^y returned to office & wrote letters etc — Meeting parties — Went to Castle

and told Mrs Watson to prepare rooms for the Countess of Dunmore
Contracted for masonry of Gisla Bridge with Murdo McIver for £10- and
with Alex^r Ross for masonry of Murdos cottage at the Creed for £7 to be
pointed with lime — Went over the Castle to see what Bell hanging & Gas
fitting is required etc etc

Wednesday 23

At office writing dispatches for Steamer till 4 P.M. when she sailed Sent
80 head of Cattle & 7 Horses to Southill by Steamer 6/- each to be paid for
carriage to Glasgow — Called on Rev^d Mr Watson who is very ill, and his
mind rather disturbed about his farms, told him to compose himself that I
hoped we might still agree — Engaged at Mr Scobies a/cs with Mr Callender
— Meeting parties at office etc etc

Thursday 24

At office all day writing letters, going over the monthly accounts — Writing
Minutes of reference regarding Scaliscro farm and writing Mr McAulay
Linshader on the subject — Went over Sheddens a/c as made out by the
Valuators appointed by the Sheriff — Went over arrangements of Farmers
Society & lists of Prizes for Shew — Went to Castle & walked over the
Building and grounds etc

Friday 25

Went to the Castle and pointed out to Alex^r McRae how the Embanking in
front was to be finished off — arrangements of Walks etc Arranged several
matters with Mr Howitt — Proceeded to Callanish, crossed over to Linshader
& had conversation with Mr McAulay on Scaliscro reference and gave him
the papers — Proceeded to head of Loch Roag, inspected House building for
piper — Walked over Road to Loch Morskill now completed — Proceeded
to Kean Reasort and arrived there at 10 P.M. —

Saturday 26 July

Inspected work done at Kean Reasort, water way cut to house levelling in
front of Cottage, Sheep Draining doing in the hills etc Went to Glen
Handwick with the Sheep drainer and shewed him what should be done there
— Took boat at Loch Langavate and proceeded along it to the North end then
along the river flowing into a second loch which it merely passes thro' to
a third & a fourth Got the boat thro them all but not without a little trouble
— These lochs & found^s seem to be good Spawning ground. Got home at
one A.M.

Monday 28 July

At office going over corrispondence — Meeting various parties from the Country, Rev^d Mr Watson Uig regarding alteration of boundaries asked by him for his farm, and stated that he would not pay his rent till the marches were altered. I told him that nothing would or could be done for him till the rent was paid, and then if it was found that the marches could be altered without injuring the neighbouring farms the matter would be considered — He still holds out against paying his rent — Met Mr Callender regarding payment of Mr Scobies accounts — Mr Munro etc etc — Examining monthly accounts — Arranging various matters with Howitt etc —

Tuesday 29 July

Went to office and met parties — Measured Misses Crichtons feu to settle dispute between them & John M^{c}kenzie — Attended meeting of Water Co^y — Went over accounts with Mr Callender — Saw Mr Munro regarding Alex. M^{c}kenzies accounts and offered to refer them to the Sheriff — Went to the Castle and inspected works doing there such as levelling around Castle repairing old laundry & fitting up same for dairy etc — Gave out plait & wine. Received Lady Dunmore, Lady Susan Murray & Captn Murray who arrived at the Castle from Harris — Dined & spent the evening with them —

Wednesday 30 July

Went to office and met various parties. Called on Mr Callander who is to leave today — Went to the Castle and walked over Gardin, Rosery, Grounds & Castle with Lady Dunmore & party Accompanied them to Stornoway to shop — Writing dispatches for Steamer till 4 P.M. Sent by her a lot of Cattle & Horses for Falkirk — At office going over Cash Account — Reading Sir John McNeills report etc etc —

Thursday 31

Went to the office, met various parties settled accounts — Went to Aignish Farm and fixed where new Shed to be built by tenant is to be placed etc — Proceeded to Garabost and there settled with Work people who are now all discharged, except the foreman & burner the latter goes by next Steamer, and the former remains for a short time in charge of the work

... is not required to be case
but £10 if there - Meeting
various parties + going ove
to months a/cs, preparing
... for

Friday 29 Aug.
... to office and was engaged
... Mr Rodk McKenzie's report on ...
... of Poors Accounts - Meeting ...
... to Court House and gave ...
Several Cases to Substantia
registration Claims - 15 ne...
... were enrolled - Attend...
... of Parochial Board
... to office and was eng...
... a/cs Meeting parties +
... to Mason Hall to get ...
... belonging to the ...
moved -

Saturday 30 Aug.
... to the office met parties - ...

Friday 1 August

Saw George McLeod regarding fishing — Went to office and met parties — Wrote letters — Attended meeting of Parochial Board where I was detained the greater part of the day   Returned to office and wrote to Tacksmen in arrear of rent to pay up —

Saturday 2 August

At office meeting parties Mr Munro regarding leases & recovery of arrears — Registration Court etc — Settling accounts & writing letters — Went to Castle and inspected Works doing there in pointing building, clearing away behind and making up in front of Castle etc etc Arranged various matters with Mr Ritchie & Mr Howitt etc — Drove to Callanish & Back [*sic*] to shew my wife & friends the Drewid Stones etc —

Monday 4 August

Arranged several matters with G McLeod Went to Ordinance office with Captⁿ Burnaby to examine plans — Met several parties at office Mr Banks Letterewe, Alexander Aignish, Mr Hutchinson etc etc — Attended meeting of Water Co^y — Had meeting with Mr Munro on various subjects — Writing letters for Packet Inspected house intended for Sailors home with Dr Millar — Examined plans of Loch Morskill Cottage with Howitt — Sent Bowie to Luiskintyre to purchase some Highland Stock at Mr McRae's sale etc

Tuesday 5 August

Went to office and met parties, wrote letters to Mr Gerrie about Tolsta Road instructions for McMillan about foot path to Kean Reasort etc. Went to Castle and inspected Works there — Proceeded to Soval and attended meeting of the Parochial Board of Lochs — Revised the Roll of Paupers, and ordered the Collectors & Inspectors Accounts to be ready for next meeting etc —

Wednesday 6

Received Steamer letters and prepared dispatches for her diparture at 4. Arranged various matters with Mr Cameron before he left — Also with Angus McLeod the keeper from Kean Reasort — Wrote J.McDonald about securing timber purchased at Loch Roag & Shawbost — Arranged with Mr A. McIver to go to Tolsta to settle with labourers at Road & take stock of meal there — Went to Goathill thence by Stewartfield & Stainish having appointed to meet parties —

Thursday 7

Went to office and was engaged there meeting parties, and writing letters to tenants in arrear of rent — Was glad to receive intelligence of the safe arrival of the Emigrant ships at Quebec, Communicated the same to the Rev^d Mr Campbell Uig & to others interested — Had meeting of Com^{ee} of Parochial Board to audit Collectors & Inspectors accounts, agreed to appoint Mr Rod^k Mackenzie to examine the accounts — Arranged various matters with Mr Ritchie — Went over part of grounds & Gardin with him — Went over Castle with Mrs Watson & Howitt and arranged various matters — Went to Square inspected work shops etc —

Friday 8 August

Arranged various matters with McIntosh regarding Holm & Sand^k Hill Farms, he seems anxious to become tenant of Holm, would give £50 for the first five years & £60 for the rest of the lease — He would not require any additions or great repairs done to the Steading but merely to make them wind & water tight — He would require £100 to assist in stocking the farm for which he would pay 5 per cent. He is a Steady respectable man & a good farmer — At office writing letters to various persons, meeting parties and going over & Settling accounts. Went to the Castle in the evening and walked over part of ground gave instructions to W^m McKay Bowie etc

Saturday 9 Aug^t

Arranged with Mr A McIver about disposal of Des^t Meal at Tolsta — At office all day writing letters and going over accounts — Also meeting parties — Went to Castle and inspected what was doing there, in dressing grounds etc

Monday 11 Aug^t

Went to the office and arranged various matters — Proceeded to Callanish & there took boat for Reef — Inspected the fence now building between the Farms of Reef and Kneep — Met John McRae the tenant of Reef and the Constables and tenants of Kneep, arranged dispute between them regarding boundaries, and fixed the line of fence to be built, Kneep to get compensation for the small portion taken off & added to Reef — Met the Rev^d Mr Watson who came to complain of Mitchell not keeping his cattle on the part of the farm alotted to him by Mr W — Told ground officer to warn Mitchell that if he did not attend to Mr Watson's instructions he would lose his holding being Mr Watson's subtenant — Called on Kenneth S[t]ewart to arrange about his marches, also on Mr McAulay Linshader to push him regarding the Scaliscro reference

Tuesday 12 Aug^t

At office meeting parties, arranged with Mr Alexander Robertson to send his Schooner Fortitude with a cargo of Kelp from Lochs to Glasgow @ 7/6 a Kelp ton, as same may turn out by bills of sales and bring back 50 tons of coal @ 6/- per ton — Went to meeting of Gas Co^y where I was detained for four hours going over accounts and transactions of the Co^y, which are so unsatisfactory so far as the manager is concerned that the Directors unanimously agreed to suspend him and to advertise for a successor. Returned to office and was engaged with Alex^r Aignish going over his rental a/cs etc With Angus Scobie for Work done in Mr Scobies time & with Alex M^{c}kenzie regarding pipers Cottage Sheddens a/cs etc Called on Mr Munro & went over papers in Urquharts Case with him etc etc —

Wednesday 13 Aug^t

Went to office and received Steamer dispatches answered same — Attended meeting of Water Co^y and discharged Wilson as Manager — Settled freight a/cs with Mr Gair — Met various parties Arranged with Mr Gerrie about Uig & Tolsta Road, also Loch Reasort Bridle Road — Went to Castle and walked over it with Mrs Watson & Mr Howitt and arranged what was to be done before the family came Walked over part of grounds and gave directions to Gardiners etc Went over & checked various a/cs

Thursday 14

Went to office & met various parties vizt Mr McRae Ness, Mr J.R. McIver, Mr Munro, etc arranged various matters — Proceeded to the West side, and on the way encountered a heavy fall of rain or rather a water spout, which damaged the Road considerably, it was confined to a mile or two there being no rain either at Stornoway or Barvas — Called at the Manse of Barvas — Proceeded to Shader & there met Mr McDonald, inspected the Drainage Works which are all but finished & may be done this week — Called at Galson & arranged with Mr McPherson to send in meat for the Castle — Inspected the Drainage Works at North Galson which are also finished — Arranged various matters & Proceeded to Swanabost where I remained for the night —

Friday 15

Went to South Dell called at the Free Manse — Inspected drainage works at Dell Mill which can be finished in the course of a week — Saw the miller about paying up his arrears of rent — Also Alex^r Murray Dell who is year after year falling deeper in arrear, he is now more than 5 years rent behind — Went to Cross Manse & Church, inspected both buildings which are much out of repair — Took note of the repairs required to be done to the Manse to make it comfortable Went over the whole of the drainage works at Ness, what is unfinished could be all completed in the course of a few days could the people be got to work but this is almost impossible — The Crops on the new land are beautiful and a few of the Crofters are still trenching on their own account — There are signs of potatoe blight almost every where

Saturday 16

Walked over the line of proposed road between Ness and Tolsta, there are nearly 100 men at present at work on this road at the Ness end — They are paid at the rate of 1/- per yard of finished roadway one half in Destitution Meal and the other half Credited in their rents — Let several sections of the road to Contractors & placed McMillan (who superintended the Uig Road) as foreman between Ness & Tolsta — The Tolsta people are by no means so keen for the work as the Ness men, and it is ill to get them to do any work — Returned by Gress & got home at 11 P.M.

Monday 18 Aug^t

Went to office and was engaged writing letters for Packet, meeting parties etc, Settled a/cs with several people — Went to the Castle and walked over the house with Mr Howitt & Mrs Watson, arranged several things to be done before family arrive — Walked over grounds and walks with Mr Ritchie — Went to Square and arranged with Bowie to get meat & fish for Castle — saw Rev^d Mr McLean Coll who wishes now to proceed to America & hopes Sir James will give what he formerly offered, delayed to give him any answer till he sees Sir James —

Tuesday 19 Aug^t

Went to office and was engaged the greater part of the day looking over corrispondence with Wilson & papers connected with the Castle building to obtain information required by Edin^h agents — going over accounts of Cattle sold at Falkirk being 132 head — The original estimated cost here was

71 Cows	@ 34/-	£120.14
40 Greys	@ 16/-	32. 0
Horses	@ 30/-	31.10
Expence of sending to Falkirk		60.17
		£245. 1
Sum realized		218. 2.0
Loss		£ 26.19

Also 80 Cattle sent to Southill Cost here

	average @ 42	£168. 0
7 Horses	@ 52/6	18. 7. 6.
Expence of transit		82.13. 0
		£ 269. 0. 6.

Meeting various parties, and writing letters — Went to Castle to see that all was ready for the reception of the family, and gave instructions on various matters — remained in Stornoway waiting the arrival of the Steamer —

Wednesday 20 Aug^t

Sir James, Lady Matheson Mrs & Miss Percival arrived at 8 A.M. per Steamer "Islay" Met them at the Pier — Went to the Castle walked over part of the Castle & grounds with Sir James gave out Plaite & some wine. Went to office and wrote letters for Steamer — Saw Captn Shelly & Mr Gair on Steamer matters — Mr Warren Post Office Inspector and had some talk with him as to postal arrangements, he proposes establishing an internal postal communication to Ness, Callanish & Soval — Explained to him the different routes & sketched lines of Roads on his map — Examining a/cs, writing letters etc Called at the Castle but did not find Sir James at Home — Saw Bowie & gave him instructions regarding supplies for Castle etc

Thursday 21 Aug^t

Went to office & met parties — Wrote letters for the Packet — Went to Castle & saw Sir James shewed him letters received by Packet — arranged various matters with Mr Howitt — Went to Square and arranged quarters for grooms — Went to house at Nursery with Sloan the gardiner and gave him possession of room there — Told Munro the miller he would be obliged to look out for another house at Martinmas as the house now occupied would be required for the Gardiner — Returned to the office to write letters & meet parties — Went to Goathill and accompanied Mr Ritchie & Gerrie over land improved there — The sea Embankment seems to stand well, the land generally seems well drained, but the crop on the new land is not very promising —

Friday 22 Aug^t

Went to office and was engaged meeting parties — going over corrispondence with J. McRae regarding his leaving Scaliscro Farm — Examining a/cs — Went to Castle to see Sir James Arranged various matters with Mr Howitt — Returned to office & wrote letters — Called on Mr Munro regarding Sheddens a/cs — and told him to write J. McRae Scaliscro threatening legal steps if he did not sign the reference formerly agreed to — at office going over Sheddens a/c with Alex Mackenzie etc etc

Saturday 23 Augus^t

Met Mr Houston & Mr McPherson Mossend at Sand^k regarding matters connected with their farms — Went to Stornoway & met Sir James, accompanied him to Castle, arranged to remove Seraphime from Chapel to Castle, and put up organ in Chapel — Went to Square & arranged various matter[s] with W^m McKay — Went to office and examined a/cs and gave instructions on various subjects — Went to Chapel & saw organ unpacked & situation for it fixed — Returned to office and received Packet letters — Met various parties Mr Gerrie, Mr McPherson, Galson, G McLeod etc etc Wrote letters to go by Steamer and parties in Country —

Monday 26 Aug^t

Went to office and arranged various matters — Went to Castle and Counted over wine in both Cellars to Butler — Proceeded to Kean Reasort with Sir James. Walked from Loch Morskill along line for footpath marked off by Mr Gerrie, but which Sir James did not approve of being rather round about — Got to the Cottage at 8 P.M.

Tuesday 26 Aug^t

Gave instructions to Angus McLeod as directed by Sir James not to go on with foot path as now laid out but to make it passable as far as first stream and to improve the crossing place at same — Measured rooms of Cottage for carpits and compared inventory with articles in House — Left the Cottage at 11 A.M. and examined the ground towards Loch Morskill with Sir James in order to ascertain the best line for a path — Sir James wished the line to be kept as streight as possible and fixed the general direction of it but arranged to send Mr Gerrie back to go over it and mark it off more particularly — Arranged various matters with Alex^r M^ckenzie at Kean Loch as to the Pipers cottage — Got home at 6 P.M.

Wednesday 27 Aug^t

Wrote out Memorandum of an agreement for Revd Ewen McLean promising that Sir James should pay him thro the Colonial Com^{ee} of the Free Church £50 per annum for three years on condition that he remained with the Lews Emigrants as their Pastor in the Eastern Townships of Lower Canada — Gave him six months salary £25 in advance, and £12 to pay his passage to Quebec, the Free Church are to pay the passage money of his family — Writing letters and meeting parties — Went to the Castle to see Sir James — arranged various matters with Mr Howitt Went to Square saw stable work shops etc — Saw Steamer off — Went to office and prepared information wanted by Mr Munro for Claims of Registration lodged by him, Called on him with same etc —

Thursday 28 Aug[t]

Went to office and arranged various matters met parties — Attended the Court being cited as a jury man — Went to Episcopal Chapel with Sir James to see organ now fitting up — Called with him to see M[c]Masters School & the Rev[d] Mr M[c]Grigor — Accompanied Sir James to the Square saw byres & pony sent by John M[c]Donald — Met Howitt and arranged for getting articles wanted for Kean Reasort   Contracted with Angus M[c]Lean to do the Mason work of Gisla Bridge for £12 the parties who formerly Contracted for the work not having gone on with it — Saw Gerrie & discribed to him the direction of foot path to Kean Reasort wished by Sir James to be laid off & to proceed there tomorrow but to wait on Sir James to take his instruction. Agreed with Alex. M[c]Kenzie Jn[r] to remove the Zink House to Loch Morskill, he to take it to pieces but we to furnish the carts and he to put if up again, do the whole workmanship & find materials except the papering for £8 if the Zink is not required to be taken off but £10 if it is — Meeting various parties & going over last months a/cs, preparing leases etc

Friday 29 Aug[t]

Went to office and was engaged going over Mr Rod[k] M[c]kenzie's report on Insp[s] & Coll[s] of Poors Acount — Meeting parties   Went to Court House and gave evidence in several cases to substantiate registration claims — 15 new voters were enrolled — Attended meeting of Parochial Board — Returned to office and was engaged examining a/cs   Meeting parties etc — Went to Mason Hall to get globe & maps belonging to Sir James removed —

Saturday 30 Aug[t]

Went to the office met parties — Went to the Castle waited on Sir James saw what was doing by tradesmen— Went to Stables arranged various matters — Returned to the office wrote letters for Steamer   Arranged about securing Flax Crop at Holm — Went over various Shopkeepers a/cs and ordered them to be paid — Had meeting with J. M[c]Rae Scaliscro who still refuses to sign the reference if his sub tenants are not made parties to it — This I object to as he is responsible for his sub tenants —

104.18.4	5.4.3	100.16.5.	6.11.7
79.2.6	3.3.3	49.12.6 -	3.0.11
50.8.6	3.3.0	20.7.11 -	6.8.6
76.4.0	2.10.9 -	10.17.2 -	1.8.6
57.17.10	2.12.7	5.10.0 -	1.19.3
31.6.0	3.9.6	8.15.0	7.17.10

e are two or three desparate
acters in Stornish who refuse
to rent & who must be ejected
home. at 11 P.M. the

Thursday 11 Sep.
t to office, had meeting with
Mr. Hutchinson about the & his
nds taking Aline farm after
tenants lease is out — He stated
they were prepared to offer
which he considered it would
proprietors interest to accept
would be converting the ground
r deer forest, and by clearing
Sheep would increase the deer

Monday 1 Sept[r]

At office met various parties among others Mr E M[c]Iver who stated that he was to do all the improvements required at Gress at his own expence and not to ask the proprietor to lay out any money if the rent was left at the old rate £90 — If this is to be agreed to on the part of the proprietor the improvements should be particularly specified to the extent in value of say £400 to £500 and to be done within a certain period — Went over monthly accounts — Attended a meeting of the Gas Co[y] directors to fix on a new manager. Wrote to Laidlaw with the testimonials of three parties that he might see them and appoint the most suitable Went to Mr Munro's office with Alexander Aignes and got him to sign Dft of new lease — made several arrangements for Cattle Shew. Went to Castle to see Sir James. Examined what was doing about Castle — Returned to Stornoway & went to the Mason Hall to attend lottery of Masons picture which was got by one of the sappers —

Tuesday 2 Sept[r]

Went to office — Met parties and wrote letters — Went to Castle and called for Sir James — Saw what was doing by tradesmen at & about Castle — Went to Cattle Shew where remained all day — There was a good Shew of Ayrshire Cattle & work Horses by the Farmers, but a great falling off in Highland Stock — The Shew of Sheep was very poor as usual — none of the large sheep farmers having brought forward stock — Dined with the Club at the Lews Hotel Sir James in the Chair —

Wednesday 3 Sep[r]

Went to office and arranged various matters — Called on D[r] Millar about house now building by him at Arch[d] M[c]Donalds feu Bayhead, he consents to give up the building and will sell the property to Sir James after the death of the old M[c]Donald — Went to the Castle and made arrangements for conveying the Zink house to Morskill. Accompanied Sir James, Hon[ble] Mr Ellice & Capt[n] Ellice to the Patent Slip Custom Ho etc — Had meeting with Mr Ritchie & Mr M[c]Donald — Attended meeting of Gas Co[y] and appointed Mr Anderson of Forres manager of the Gas & Water Works — Prepared dispatches for Steamer — Had meeting with Mr Munro, M[c]Leod Valtos, A Robertson as to kelp vessel etc

Thursday 4

Did no business being the fast day — Called at the Castle to see Sir James

Friday 5 Sept^r

Went to Stables to arrange for Conveyances to go to Callanish — Went to office and met various parties Mr McLeod Valtos, A Robertson Mr Munro, Captn Burnaby — Sir James called to sign Charter for L.H. Commissioners — Wrote letters to various parties — Accompanied Sir James to Luerbost — Crossed the loch to Swordale which is rather a pretty place & where grows the only natural wood in the Lews. Sir James talked of enclosing the wood Took boat for Croigary and walked to Soval Attended a meeting of the Parochial Board & laid on an assessment of 1/8 per pound of rent one half to be paid by landlord & one half by tenant — Walked over ground trenched & drained at Soval, Sir James wishes the fence to be repaired and a few additional drains to be put in to dry the land — returned home at 7 P.M.

Saturday 6 Sept^r

Went to the Episcopal Chapel and examined the building which is in good order, it may be pointed and whitewashed, asked masons to give in estimate — Told Mr Ritchie to Contract for Cutting a drain round it — Went to office and wrote letters Met parties — Was occupied during the forenoon with a J.P. Court — Attended Church in the afternoon — Called at the Castle to see Sir James — Arranged about sending boat to Loch Creed etc

Monday 8 Sep^r

Went to the office and met parties arranged various matters — Went to the Castle and saw party off to Callanish & Kean Reasort — Returned to office had meeting with Major Houstoun about pensioners — With Mr Campbell the Tax Surveyor, Captn Burnaby etc Wrote to Ground officers fixing days of meeting with tenants in each parish to pay their rents etc Wrote letters to various parties Attended Church — Returned to office and wrote letters for Packet applying in all directions to get vessels to go for kelp to West Side but cannot succeed — Arranged various matters with Mr Ritchie Bowie etc

Tuesday 9 Sep^r

Had meeting with Rev^d Mr Leid about a School Master for his Parish — Proceeded to Garabost to Collect the Point rents, met the tenants of Portnaguran who have their rents pretty well paid up, The tenants of Port Vollar the one half of whom pay well, some of the remaining half do what they can to pay, and a few seem to shew no wish to pay in particular Dond McLeod Constable who was summoned out of his holding last term, and tho' continued in it did not appear today to pay his rent. Wrote Mr Munro to get him ejected and secure his stock for the rent. Met the tenants of Aird several of whom, who were much in arrear, were summoned out of their holdings, but on condition of being allowed to cast peat granted a joint bill (now due) for the amount of their arrears, which they this day retired — There are a few desparate characters in this farm — Met the tenants of Sheshader, some of whom paid their rents and others paid nothing — There are some parties in possession of Crofts on this farm much in arrear and who can never pay, two old men & one or two widows, these must be deprived of their large Crofts and put on smaller patches of land which they agree to — The people of this farm complain of being over rented — I must visit this farm the first leasure time I can command to arrange matters — Met the tenants of Shulishader, several of whom made no payments tho' rather in arrear, they have a good stock & can pay in the course of the season. A considerable amount of drainage money has been laid out in improving the crofts of this farm and they complain of the amount of interest chargeable — The Results of this days work are as follows

	No of tenants	Total Rent	Average Rent	Collection in Cash & Cattle	Avge Arrears
Portnaguran	16	£39. 7. 5.	£2. 9.10.	£32.16. 6.	£1.11/-
Port Vollar	13	41.18. 3.	3. 4. 5.	19. 6. 0.	4.14/9
Aird	16	54. 4. 6.	3. 7. 9.	31.18. 0.	4.15/4
Sheshader	20	81.12. 4.	4. 1. 7.	58. 9.11.	5.14/9
Shulishader	21	78.19. 9.	3.15. 3.	24. 6. 1.	4. 7/8

Returned home at 2 A.M. — The above townships are all fishing villages except Shulishader

Wednesday 10 Sep[r]

Returned to Garabost and collected the rents of that Township, which upon the whole are pritty well paid up principally on account of the employment given at the Brick & Tile work, there are a few desparate Characters on the farm — Went over the tenants of Upper & Lower Bayble, in these townships there are some of the best doing tenants on the estate, owning large Wick boats with a full complement of nets, and who pay their rents most punctually, there are also in these farms some of the poorest and most desparate, old men who have no families, having lost them or been disleted by them, and numbers of widows, who occupy lots that they cannot pay — There are also a few worthless characters who have no wish to pay — This may be better arranged by next term in depriving such of land & giving those who cannot pay smaller lots — The tenants on the new land in these townships seem to be doing well — Went over the Tenants of Knock and Swordale — The tenants of the former farms have been paying up their arrears pritty well this season — Six of the best tenants of the latter place were drowned last year, and it is to be feared the arrears of this farm will greatly increase — The Result of this days work shews as follows

	Tenants	Total Rent	Average Rent	Collection	Average Arrears
Garabost	62	£180.14. 7.	£2.18. 3.	£57.13. 8.	£2. 7. 2.
Up Bayble	32	111. 3. 3.	3. 9. 5.	82.12.10.	1.18. 8.
L. Bayble	42	134.18. 9.	3. 4. 3.	100.16. 5.	6.11. 7.
Knock	25	79. 2. 6.	3. 3. 3.	49.12. 6.	3. 0. 11.
Swordale	16	50. 8. 6.	3. 3. 0.	20. 7.11.	6. 8. 5.
Melbost	30	76. 4. 0.	2.10. 9.	10.17. 2.	1. 8. 5.
Branahui	22	57.17.10.	2.12. 7.	5.10. 0.	1. 19. 3.
Stainish	9	31. 6. 0.	3. 9. 6.	8.15. 0.	7.17.10.

There are two or three desperate Characters in Stainish who refuse to pay rent & who must be ejected. Got home at 11 P.M. etc

Thursday 11 Sep[r]

Went to office, had meeting with Rev[d] Mr Hutchinson about he & his friends taking Aline farm after Mr Stewarts lease is out — He stated that they were prepared to offer £50 which he considered it would be the proprietors interest to accept as it would be converting the ground into a deer forest, and by clearing it of Sheep would increase the deer — I could make no answer till I had consulted with Sir James but that I did not think Stewarts lease was out till 1854 — Went over the Prop[y] tax returns with the Surveyor and accompanied him to the Castle to See Sir James, when he agreed to accept of a reduced rental return in proportion to the Amounts received. Arranged various matters at the office and with Ritchie Howitt and Bowie — Again saw Mr Hutchinson in Sir James room, when Sir James stated that he would expect the present rent for Aline Farm, but that nothing could be done till the indurance of Stewarts lease was determined. The taking of the tenants stock at the end of the lease was also an obstacle — Went to Soval to collect the Lochs rents and was accompanied so far by Major Houston & Mr Hutchinson — Met the tenants of Raenish and went over the a/c of each tenant — This Township was much in arrear but they are paying up pritty well except some desparate parties whoes lots were let to other parties — Settled with the tenants of Crosbost who all pay well being good fishermen, tho' not considered very good Characters — Also with the people of Balallan &

Airybrough. The greater part of the rent of these farms has been paid for the last two years in Kelp, which paid the expence of making last year but on which there will be a considerable loss this year, as the price is much lower than I was laid to expect in the beginning of the season — However several have been enabled to pay rents that otherwise would remain in arrear — Many of the Balallan people shew a great wish to pay and are improving their Crofts on account of which I told all who paid up that they would get leases — The result of today is as follows

	Tenants	Total Rent	Average Rent	Collection Cattle & Kelp	Average Arrears
Raenish	48	£131	£2.14. 2.	£108.19. 5.	£3. 1.10.
Crosbost	27	60	2. 4. 6.	42.11. 7.	6. 8.
Balallan	62	178.10.-	2.17. 7.	65.	1.18. 5.
Airybrough	14	19.15.	1. 8. 2.	18.10. 6.	0.13.10.

Friday 12 Sep^r

Met the people of Luerbost some of whom are still in arrear but the greater part have paid up pritty well for the last year Also settled with the tenants of Cromore, Gravir, Marivig, Kershader & Calbost, all fishing vill[i]ages and good payers of rent tho' occupying the worst land in the Lews, they make well of the herring fishing at Stornoway & Wick having good boats and nets, almost every tenant is a part owner of a boat It is a pleasure to see the readiness & goodwill with which these people pay their rents except a few at Gravir Luerbost and Kershader who are deprived of land and let it to parties able and willing to pay rent The results shewn by this days work are as follows

	Tenants	Rent	Avge Rent	Average Arrears	Collection
Leurbost	57	134.19	2. 7. 2.	0.17. 7.	56.15.11.
Cromore	21	84. 1.	4. 0. 1.	1. 5. 6.	60. 4. 2.
Marivig	12	34. 0.	2.16. 8.	19. 1.	24.19. 8.
Calbost	10	30.	3. 0. 0.	12. 9.	29. 4. 8.
Gravir	32	86. 9. 6.	2.14. 0.	1.16. 4.	63. 6. 6.
Kershader	10	32.	3. 4. 0.	2.18. 6.	19. 5. 3.

Saturday 13 Sep[r]

Met the tenants of Laxay who upon the whole are good payers tho' there may be one or two exceptions, also the tenants of Koes some of whom are behind but promise to pay up — The tenants of Gary Vard and Hawbost — Old Duncan M[c]Lellan occupies one half of the latter farm but at the Martinmas term his holding is to be reduced one half, he has paid up part of his arrears this season. Settled with the tenants of Grimshader and deprived some of land and let it to others — The townships settled with today are as follows

	No	Rent	Average	Arrears	Collection
Laxay	25	71. 2.10.	2.16.11.	0.11.10.	22. 0. 5.
Koes	15	50	3. 6. 8.	2. 0.11.	30.12. 6.
Grimshader	12	35	2.18. 5.	2. 1. 1.	20.18. 0.
Hawbost	8	40. 1	5. 1. 0.	6. 7. 0.	17. 4. 6.
Gary Vard	7	22	3. 2.10.	1. 1.11.	15.14. 4.
Achmore	13	28. 7. 6.	2. 3. 7.	1. 4. 4.	15.16. 8.

Lochs is the only parish in which the land has not been relotted and the people almost to a man express a great wish that this should be done — Mr Cameron will begin the work so soon as he gets the Cattle off his hands — I had a call today from Mr Stewart who is most anxious to get a renewal of his lease of Aline which he says expires next Whitsunday — He says he is prepared to give an increase of rent, but this will very much depend on how the Harris March is fixed — Taking all matters into consideration I would be disposed to recommend Aline to be continued as a sheep farm and Stewart the tenant as his rent is sure, besides he stocks his ground so very lightly that the deer have a good share of the grass. If he is not continued his Stock must be taken at a valuation and what is afterwards to be done with them is a question if the farm is to be cleared for deer, as they will not all be marketable — It would be a disadvantage if the ground were again placed under sheep at any future period to have to rear a new Stock on it, in the event of its not letting as a shooting, which is more probable than its not letting as a sheep farm — I consider the present arrangement is the best that can be made, at all events it gives two strings to the bow — Left Lochs much pleased with the people seeing that they had done their best to pay their rents and upwards of 100 tenants closed their accounts — The greater number of the rest promise to do the same by Martinmass by which term I intend to revisit the Parish —

Monday 15 Sept[r]

Went to the office and met various parties, Mr Houston, Mr Munro etc etc Accompanied Sir James & Mr Clark Hopman to ground near Gas Work which he wishes to rent for the purpose of erecting a Haddock Smoking House etc — Attended poor law meeting, revised Roll of Point district with the aid of the Constables — Adjourned to this day week — Had meeting at Mr Munro's office with Sir James regarding papers to be sent to Edin[h] in M[c]Nabs case — Arranged that all papers should be sent to the Edin[h] agents leaving the matter in their hands, which to produce — Was engaged at the office till one A.M. writing letters and preparing dispatches — Chartered the Schooner "Jessie" to go to load kelp from the West Side for Glasgow, the kelp from Loch Roag to be at the rate of 10/- per kelp ton and that from the outside coast to be at the rate of 12/- per ton — Attended lecture by Mr M M[c]Iver on the great Exhibition etc etc

Tuesday 16 Sept[r]

Went to the office and was engaged writing letters, settling a/cs and meeting parties — Wrote Missive of lease for Mr Clark for two acres of land let to him near the Gas Work at £4 per acre, purchased coal for Castle — Arranged various matters with Howitt, Bowie & Ritchie — Went to Callanish accompanied by Sir W[m] Davidson & Major Percival — Met there the tenants of Breascalate Callanish Garynahine Tolsta Chuilish & Dune Carloway — The people of three first townships are very industrious and generally pay their rents if work can be had in the Country and at kelp making. The kelp from this district not having been shipped yet I could not settle with the people, which when put to their Credit will clear the greater Part of the arrears against them — The Townships settled with today are as follows —

	No. Tenants	Rent	Avge Rent	Collection	Avge Arrears
Garynahine	12	£ 43. 8. 9.	£3.12. 6.	£8. 7. 4.	£2.10. 8.
Breascalate	38	112. 7. -.	2.19. 1.	31. 2. 0.	1. 3. 4.
Tolsta Chuilish	21	73.15.	3.10. 2.	29.19. 2.	2. 2. 2.
Dune Carloway	16	56. 5. 6.	3.10. 4.	12.15. 2.	4. 7.11.

The people of the two last named townships are not so industrious and are more in arrear of rent, I gave them notice that if such was not paid up by Martinmas the farms would be apt to be cleared for sheep for which they are more answerable than for tillage — Doune Carloway if added to the improved land at that place would make a good farm, without an outrun for stock the tenant of the improved land cannot pay a rent and I am very doubtfull of Humphreys success — 10 families emigrated from Callanish & 10 families from Tolsta Chuilish all of whom were very poor & much in arrear of rent, the small patches of land they occupied are still vac[c]ant and should be continued so, these places having been overcrouded.

Wednesday 17 Sep^r

Proceeded up Loch Roag by boat to Kean Langavate, Walked to the Parish School House where we got rooms and put up there not being on very good terms with Mr Watson, besides we will have our time more to ourselves & be less disturbed here, and as we have carried our own provisions with us and pay for any trouble we give we can be more at ease than living on Mr Watson who grudged the expence we put him to — None of the people being here to meet me tho' they got notice some days ago sent messengers in all directions to tell of my arrival — A few made their appearance during the evening but brought little or no money — I sent them back to warn their neighbours to come tomorrow with Cash or Cattle to pay their rents —

Thursday 18 Sept^r

Met the people of Braenish a few of whom pay their rents & the greater portion are in arrear — some very desparate having already parted with almost all their stock to pay their rents, on account of the long continuance of low prices they have reduced their stock much to meet the demand for rent & meal — Those who pay most are engaged in fishing lobsters etc — This township must be cleared at no distant day if the price of Cattle does not improve & the potatoe crop does not succeed — met the people of Islivick which tho' a small place the same remark applies as to Braenish — There are two desparate people on this farm one with a family of 10 who has neither sheep or cow and is £21.13.5. in arrear of rent, he refused to emigrate on the plea of having no clothing for his children. The other has been confined to bed for 7 years with white swelling in his knee, I have often wished him to come to Stornoway to get his leg amputated, he is £12 — in arrear — The rest of the tenants are pritty well paid up — Went over their accounts with the tenants of Mangersta who are also much in arrear, but who occupy much better land for tillage and have larger stocks of Cattle & Sheep than the other two farms & on that account I have better hopes of their reviving — Next called the tenants of Carnish few of whom appeared and the few who did paid little of nothing. 6 families from this farm emigrated this year and the remaining tenants despair of being continued in the farm as they are so much in arrear and on that account shewed no wish to pay — They are almost all desparate characters in this farm. Two or three heads of families have been confined to bed for years and there are some widows — This would make a good addition to Arderoil Farm and the sooner it is cleared the better as the present tenants will never pay a tithe of the rent — Those who are able to emigrate should be sent, and those who can not to get places elsewhere — Sent the Ground Officer with a list of the arrears to the above mentioned places and told him to take no excuse, but to bring the people with Cash or Cattle to pay their rents, that if they did not endeavour to pay the Currrent rent, and if they allowed the arrears to accumulate they must Certainly be removed — These farms stand as follows

[No headings shown]

Braenish	27	£95. 4. 1.	£3.10. 6.	£53.17. 2	£3. 9. 5.
Islivick	11	26. 8.11.	2. 8. 1.	11. 9. 6.	3. 6. 8.
Mangersta	16	71. 6. 0.	4. 9. 1.	45.11. 6.	5.13. 2.
Carnish	12	51. 3. 3.	4. 5. 3.	10. 6. 0.	12. 7.10.

Settled with a few of the people of Croulista & Valtos —

Friday 19 Sep[r]

Met the people of Carishader, Inaclate, Gisla & Ungishader who have paid up their rents by kelp making and work on the Uig Road — Met the people of Valtos some of whom are most respectable and pay their rents, others are not so & do not wish to pay — Their stock of Cattle is very much reduced, but Valtos is a good fishing port and they have got one or two Wick boats and if they were industrious they might still succeed — Next met the people of Kneep who paid little or nothing — I have lost all hope of this farm, they have little or no stock, they do nothing to earn money and their arrears are increasing year after year with their means deminishing — This farm cannot be continued on the present footing as the rent is lost & no hope of any improvement — The people who can go should Emigrate — Next met the people of Croulista & Aird Uig — Several in both these townships are much in arrear while others pay up — A deputation from each place came to me to say that there were people on both farms who could take and pay the places if some of the most desparate were deprived of land & others put in their places who could pay, that they would become jointly & severally bound for the rents — I replied that if the present arrears were paid up by Martinmas next except that due by a few very old & poor people I would recommend the proprietor to give them a short lease say 7 years to make a trial of what they proposed, on which severals came forward and made payments — This days work appears as follows

Carishader*	10	23.17. 0.	2. 7. 8.	1. 0. 0.	4. 1. 5.
Enaclate*	8	30. 0. 0.	3.15. 0.	13. 9. 9.	1. 7. 8.
Gisla*	4	17. 0. 0.	4. 5. 0.	5. 8.10.	1. 8. 4.
Ungishader*	3	14. 1. 7.	4.13.10.	3. 4. 4.	3. 1. 0.
Valtos	28	141. 8. 8.	5. 1. 0.	64.14. 4.	6.17. 5.
Kneep	17	82.15. 0.	4.17. 4.	29. 9.10.	8. 1. 2.
Croulista	18	74. 8. 0.	4. 2. 8.	37. 6. 6.	6. 2. 6.
Aird Uig	7	23.15. 0.	3. 7.10.	9. 0. 0.	4.12. 9.
Geshader*	7	26.17.-.	3.16. 7.	5.17. 9.	4.10. 6.

Those marked thus * have not yet delivered the Kelp made by them this season & they have not been C^r for the same. Called at the Manse and had some argument with Mr Watson about the payment of his rent which he still holds out against. Inspected the Manse buildings with him and find several parts of the timber quite decayed, pointed out same to Contractor and arranged with him to replace same with sound timber — Inspected the offices and find the byre stable & cart shed in such a state of ruin that it will be more satisfactory to build new ones and almost cost as little as to repair the old ones besides if any change was to take place in the living the Presbytery would at once order new offices, or Condemn the present Manse and offices, and put the proprietor to the expence of building new ones — Prepared a Plan of new Byre, Stable and Cart Shed and made Estimate of same —

Saturday 20th

Arranged with Angus McLean mason & Rod^k McLeod joiner to build new offices for the Manse and furnish all materials for the sum of £87.11.11. being 50 per cent lower that I could have expected to have got the work done for, which is accounted for by the following facts, stones are already on the ground in the old buildings, drift timber has been purchased at a low rate in the neighbourhood, and the Contractors were anxious to get the work being already engaged on the spot in repairing the Manse — Severals of the tenants of Mangersta & Braenish came forward today with Cash and Cattle in the hope of being able to keep their holdings — Mr Watson having expressed a great desire to arrange matters amicably & stated that he would sacrifice £40 for the sake of pease — I wrote out a Minute which I got him & Mitchell to sign referring the valuation of the portion of the farm occupied by Mitchell & payable by him to Mr Watson to Mr Cameron and John McRae, Mr Mitchell ceding all right to the Island of Vaxay and agreeing to crop no part of the farm, Mr Watson giving him 5 acres in the glebe park for that purpose and wintering on the Glebe for his young Cattle stock. Mr Mitchell to leave the farm at Whitsunday 1852 if required to do so by Mr Watson — Both parties seemed perfictly satisfied with this arrangement and Mr Watson agreed to withdraw all claims for damages on account of the farm not being cleared on the arrangment being carried out by Mitchell — I promised Mitchell a small holding elsewhere if he performed his part of the Contract. Mitchell deserves to be treated kindly as he honestly gave up all to pay his arrears without puting the Proprietor to the expence of a sequestration — Inspected the Church of Uig and ordered some small repairs to be done to make it wind & water tight — Called at the Free Manse and there met the Rev^d Mr McLean of Tobermory a native of the Parish who has been preaching against Emigration, had a long argument with him on that subject and told him my opinion very plainly, I hope he will be more careful of what he says in future Proceeded to Barnera & met the tenants of that Island and got payments from them in Cash and Cattle — The greater part of them are engaged in the Lobster fishing and have not yet got their money for this seasons fishing — They stand as follows

	No. of Tenants	Rent	Avge Rent	Collection	Avge Arrears
Croir	8	£31.10.	£3.18. 9.	£9. 7. 0	£2. 9. 9.
Bosta	10	40. 0.	4. 0. 0.	14.18. 8.	3. 7. 3.
Tobson	20	67. 8.	3. 7. 4.	9.15. 0.	6. 11. 2.
Haclet	4	8.10.	2. 2. 6.	3.10.10.	2. 5.11.
Balligloum	5	18. 0.	3.12. 0.	1. 5. 0.	6. 9. 8.
Breaclate	3	12.15/-	4. 5.0.	6. 0. 0.	6.15. 2.

3 Families from Tobson, 1 from Haclate and 6 from Breaclate have emigrated — The remaining tenants at Haclate and Balligloum have been removed to Breaclete and the lands formerly occupied by them can be added to Mr McAulays & Stewarts farms — There are a number of poor people at Tobson who I fear cannot pay rent and must be deprived of land — I hope the other Townships in Barnera will do better — Called at Earshader and met the small tenants of that place and Croulivig they stand thus

[No headings shown]

Earshader	4	£14. 0. 0.	3.10.	3. 2. 0	2. 4. 8.
Croulivig	3	12. 5. 0.	4. 1.8.	7.18. 0.	2.17. 2.

Proceeded to Callanish and got home at 2 A.M.

Monday 22

Went to the office and was engaged reading letters — Major Houstoun called and paid for Cattle sent him from McLennan Kean Reasort — Had meeting with Mr Pirrie regarding a/c claimed by McNab from Water Co^y which I refused to sustain — Had meeting with various parties, settled several a/cs — Attended a meeting of the Parochial Board where I was detained for five hours revising the Roll with the advice of the Constables, and at other business — Returned to the office going over offers for repairs of Coll Steading & preparing for leaving for Ness — Saw Mr D L Mackenzie and offered him freight of kelp from Loch Roag @ 10/- per ton & to take over some lime & slates there for Uig Manse, promised to give me an answer on my return — Called at the Castle saw Sir James and gave him Cash book, arranged about sending R B B notes to Mr Matheson Glasgow — Returned to office, wrote letters etc — Left for Ness at 8 P.M. and arrived at Swanabost at 1 A.M. —

Tuesday 23 Sep^r

At Swanabost all day going over their rent accounts with the tenants of Eoropy, Five Penny, Knockaird, Callivol, Skegersta & Lionel — got little or no cash tho' the people of this district are much in arrear of rent, they are chiefly employed in the Co[*l*]d & Ling fishing and for the last few years since the failure of the potatoe crop have drawn almost their whole earnings in meal from the Curers — They do not go so much to Wick as the fishermen from the other districts and own no large boats — The three townships first above mentioned occupy the extreme north point of the Island which is good soil but the people are very poor have little or no stock, many of them particularly in Eoropy & Five penny are old men without families or widows who have no possible way of paying rents & it is a difficult question what to do with them, the proprietor can derive no benefit from continuing them on these farms — If the point were cleared it would make a very good grazing and could be easily fenced but would not realize the present rent charged — I have better hopes of the other townships as most of the families in them have each a member fishing & if their crops turn out anything good of which there is a prospect this season they can pay their rents by the fishing — After going over the a/cs of each tenant in the farm I called in the whole township and addressed them stating the total amount of arrears against them & told them it was impossible that the proprietor could allow such a state of matters to go on any longer, that if the arrears were not paid up by next Whitsunday they must prepare for a change, and that they should exert themselves in every possible way to prevent extreme measures being taken, and that those who paid should look after those who did not etc etc The state of these Townships is as follows

	No. of Tenants	Rent	Average Rent	Collection	Average Arrears
Eoropy	24	£90	£3.10.10.	£25.17.	£10.10. 1.
Fivepenny	15	49. 8.	3. 5.10.	11.19.	10.10. 3.
Knock Aird	15	54.12. 6.	3.12. 9.	8. 8.6.	9. 2.9.
Callicvol	16	39. 7.3.	2. 9. 2.	7.10. 0.	3. 4.9.
Skegersta	16	45.12. 5.	2.17. 0.	18.12.12.[*sic*]	4. 3.2.
Lionel	32	93. 8.8.	2.18. 4.	37. 7. 0.	4. 6.1.

Wednesday 24 Sep[r]

Met the people of Habost, Swanabost, Cross, North Dell and South Dell who are all much in arrear of Rent particularly the Dells — The greater number of the Habost & Swanabost people fish and there is some hope of getting rents from them, but I have little hope of the rest — In former times, before the fishing was begun at Ness the people paid their rents by distilling and selling whisky, the population was not then so great and the crofts were much larger some containing as much as 20 acres, which they worked with their small horses — The soil of Ness is better adapted for growing grain than any in the Lews, a small portion of their grain made into whisky paid their rent and the remainder they had for their support — They have no extent of pasture at Ness and on that account have not such a large stock as in other parts — When the times changed and whisky could no longer be made those who did not change their occupation and became fishermen are now very ill off. This class is very numerous in Ness, and there is little hope of their being able to pay rents — Ness is better adapted for Small tenants than any part of the Island, the soil being good, and if it were well cultivated would produce more food than would support the inhabitants, their crofts are larger and the rents more moderate than in other parts, and their coast abounds in fish, taking these matters into view I have some hesitation in recommending that any part of Ness should be cleared tho' I think many should be deprived of their land — Tomorrow being the Sacramental Fast day went on to Galson where I remained for the night

Habost
Swanibost
Cross   [*No figures appear against names*]
No. Dell
So. Dell
Eorodale
Quishader

Thursday 25

Went on to Barvas the people of the Borves & Shadders having gone to Ness to the Preaching which they prefer to paying rent — Called at the Manse — Proceeded to Lower Barvas and at the Free Church School there met the people of Upper & Lower Barvas Brue & Arnold, went over the account of each of the tenants in these townships and received a little money & some Cattle — The people of Upper Barvas are of a more respectable class than Lower Barvas and will strive to pay their rents — The people of Lower Barvas with the exception of a few are the most rascally set on the Property, and are much in arrear of rent, great part of which will never be recovered. Some of them would Emigrate & it would be well to get them off — The people of Brue tho' behind can pay up as they have a good stock of Cattle and Sheep — There are a few families on this farm who have been removed from Uig (Reef) and are not doing well — The people of Arnold I hope will pay up the greater part of what is against them by the term except three of four families of the name of Campbell who are noted for dishonesty and lazyness. They own some Wick boats in this township and make well of the fishing — I addressed each township as at Ness telling them that I would make another round by Martinmas by which time those who did not pay up might prepare for a change — And that if each township as a whole did not endeavour to pay up what was against it — the land might be turned to other purposes such as sheep farms — Dined with the School Master and went to the Manse for the night — the Townships gone over today appear as follows

Up Barvas
Lower Barvas   *[No figures appear against names]*
Brue
Arnold

Friday 26

Proceeded to Shawbost, and none of the people having assembled went to the Quay and examined the work going on there, which has made very considerable progress since my former visit, the people are now most anxious to get work at the Quay to pay their rents, but a few can only be employed at a time. In former years they made a point of drawing all their earnings in meal if possible but the case is now different, the people at the Quay were told that they would get one half their earnings in Destitution meal, which they are not for taking wishing the whole to be put to their rent a/c but this I do not agree to as we have meal on hand and one half of their labour is enough to be charged to rent a/c — From what has already been done Shawbost is now a safe harbour for boats and a landing can be got with any weather — They intend to fish out of this port this season. Met the people of North & South Bragor and North & South Shawbost some of whom made small payments in Cash and Cattle — The Bragors are very populous, and there are a few very respectable tenants in them who pay their rents, but the greater majority do not pay regularly are a very bad set, & many of them have no stock. The Bragors would make a good sheep farm but it would cost more than it would be worth to clear it — There are a number of old people and widows in these farms occupying land who can pay nothing — North Shawbost is one of the largest townships in the Lews, a portion of it is occupied by people removed from Uig who I hope will do better here than in their former holdings, they have much more arable land than they occupied at Uig and intend to establish a fishing here — Upwards of 100 acres of new land drained & trenched was lotted out to the small Tenants here but they are not doing well, their crops have been very bad, not being able to give the land so much manure as it would require, severals of those who took these lots emigrated and a large portion of the new land is now vaccant — Two people who took 10 acre lots wished them to be reduced the first year to 8 acres and last year to 4. One of them now wishes to give up the land — There are several in N Shawbost who I fear cannot pay rent — The South Shawbost people are better off and hope can almost all pay their rents — Gave notice that I would call on them again before Martinmas, & gave an address to each township warning them of their danger if they did not pay their rents — The Townships settled with today appear as follows

	No Tenants	Rental	Avge Rent	Coll.	Average Arrears
N. Bragor	35	£86. 5. 7.	£2. 9. 3.	15. 8. 7.	£5.14. 0.
S. Bragor	54	140. 1. 0.	2.11.10.	32.18. 0.	5.14. 1.
N. Shawbost	32	94.15. 8.	2.19. 3.	20.17. 0.	4. 5. 4.
S. Shawbost	50	133.12. 6.	2.13. 5.	32. 3. 2.	2.14. 8.
New Shawbost	21	83. 5. 6.	3.19. 3.	11. 1. 6.	7. 3. 2.

Proceeded to Dalbeg and remained there for the night —

Saturday 27 Sep[r]

At Dalbeg met two or three of the tenants of Dalmore, the greater number failed to appear, the people of this township never shewed any disp[o]sition to pay rent, and are in the greatest poverty — I have no hesitation in recommending that this township be cleared at Whitsunday next and added to Dalbeg farm which it adjoins, the people who do not emigrate may be provided for elsewhere. Several families have already left the township Some have Emigrated & others gone to other farms and there will be no difficulty in removing the rest — Met the people of Garininn who generally pay up their rents but some of them are a little in arrear this season, but which they promise soon to pay — Met the people of Borrowston who are almost all fishermen and pay pritty well except two or three who are now deprived of their land and let to others — Met the people of Upper Carloway & Knock Carloway both of which are very much in arrear, so much so that I see little hope of their being able to pay up, particularly as they have parted with the greater part of their Stock — These farms should be cleared & the people sent to America — they could be added to Doune Carloway if the small township of Kerrivick intervening were also cleared and all would make a good grazing and respectable farm — The people of Kerrivick are not so much in arrear — Addressed the people of these townships and told the people of Dal More Upper & Knock Carloway that if they did not pay up by Whitsunday I saw no prospect of their being continued in possession of these farms after that term — The State of these townships appear as follows

[No headings shown]

Dalmore	16	57	3.11. 3.	8. 3. 6.	12. 1. 3.
Garininn	16	70. 7.	4. 8. 0.	26. 4. 8.	3. 5. 3.
Upper Carloway	21	70.15.	3. 7. 4.	14.11. 0.	7. 7. 6.
Knock Carloway	17	47.15.	2.16. 2.	13. 0. 0.	6. 2. 7.
Borrowston	14	41.10.	2.19. 3.	25. 0. 0.	3.15. 8.
Kerrivick	10	36. 5.	3.12. 6.	16.12.2.	3.15. 9.

I fear Humphrey is not doing much with his farm, his crops this year and last have been very poor, and he has little or no stock on the farm, I fear he cannot pay much rent — Got home at 2 A.M.

Monday 29 Sep^r

At office reading letters, meeting parties Mr Howitt, Mr Leid Lochs to whom I paid his stipend also Rev^d Mr McRae Stornoway, received payment to a/c of rents from them — Called at Castle to see Sir James, arranged about protecting the Zink House with Brick Walls and roofing it with felt — Letters from Emigrants etc Attended meeting of the Parochial Board and was detained at it the greater part of the day — Returned to the office to write letters etc —

Tuesday 30 Sep^r

At office going over offers for finishing repairs of Coll Steading, accepted John Sheills offer for £65 — Called on Mr Munro to take his advice as to the terms of acceptance — Going over Howitts corrispondence with Mr Wilson — Had meeting with Banker on various subjects — Going over and settling monthly accounts, salaries etc — Settled Colin Morisons a/c — Writing letters etc —

Tuesday 28 Oct.

...office writing paper on
...gration. Attended a S. P.
...t. Went to Distillery to see
...paid. Went over Workshop
...ables &c. Called at Castle...
...for James. Went over
...planade House with John
...Munge & his wife and put
...under their charge to keep
...free &c. Returned to office
...anged with Rowie to
...en streets. Remove the
...pings to the grounds for
... future. Settled with John
...dies for his Contracts for
...and Hoole Moorehill Road

Wednesday 29 Oct.
...t to Milbost and saw land
...ished to be drained by Mr Housel...

Wednesday 1 Oct[r]

Arranging matters with M[c]Intosh regarding Holm farm — Going over rental a/cs Called on Mr Munro regarding various matters — Meeting parties at office — Called at Castle to see Sir James — gave notice to Laundry Maid of her discharge — Shewed Sir James state of arrears & rent Collections, and consulted him about ejecting Angus M[c]Leod Port Vollar to which he agreed — Went to stables, inspected same — Returned to office and Settled with Houston & Co[y] for work at Guirshader placed the greater part to C[r] of rents — Had meeting with Mr Milbank — Mr Ross Inspector of Poor of Lochs called with him on Mr Munro about his a/c — Had meeting with Alex M[c]kenzie regarding his a/cs when he admitted that every Item of my a/c was correct but delayed certifying it till I produced all my vouchers, one of them is in Edin[h] for which I have written — Writing letters for Steamer till 2 A.M. —

Thursday 2 Oct[r]

Went to office and was detained there till 3 P.M. endeavouring to arrange with the Rev[d] Mr Watson Uig — When there he promised that if I would give him a little indulgence in the bill due by him for Stock he would pay part of it and part of his rent as he expected to receive money for Cattle and wool sold by him — He today states that he has not recovered any part of his money and wishes to be paid his stipend, I offered him £30 or £40 if he paid the balance to a/c of rent and renewed his bill for one month — The bill was accordingly drawn out and signed but on my giving him the receipt for rent he would not receive it saying that he would not pay any sum to a/c of rent but that he would leave the money in my hands to his C[r] without putting it to any a/c till his dispute with Mitchell was arranged and I put him in possession of proper Marches — I de[c]lined taking the money on these terms and told him he was in possession of his farm as Mitchell his predicessor had it — I went with him to Mr Munro and he & I did all we could to get him to terms and pay part of his rent reminding him of his promise at Uig and his agreement with Mitchell but to no avail — On that account I retained his whole stipend with his consent & placed it to C[r] of the bill for Stock which reduces it to £10 — Wrote Mr J. M[c]Donald with bills of lading for "Jessie", settled with John Smith for Uig Road — Met various parties — Started for Coll and there met the people of North & South Tolsta. and Vatsker — The Tolsta people are much in arrear of rent and I fear can never pay — They seem a lazy indolent set & many of them shew no anxiety to pay rents — There are several fishermen among them, and Tolsta is a good fishing port, but like all others who depend entire[l]y on the Cod & Ling fishing they draw their earning in meal & shop goods and little or nothing of the produce of that labour goes to pay rent — What the fishermen pay mostly comes from Caithness — The Tolstas would make a good sheep farm if cleared, and would be an excellent addition to Gress, without being at the expence of building more Houses — If the people could or would pay I would not recommend this — I addressed them and warned them if their rents were not better paid up by Whitsunday they might look out for a change — The Vatsker people are better payers & can retain their farm at a much higher rent than one man could pay   Addressed each township stating their arrears & telling them that I intended making another round by Martin[s] and those who did not then pay would be deprived of land & if the township did not pay in whole it might be cleared — The days work appears as follows

[No headings shown]

N. Tolsta	23	£66. 5/-	£2.17. 7.	£21.10/-	£5.16/-
S. Tolsta	42	109.10. 6.	2.12. 1.	39.17. 6.	5.15/5
Glen Tolsta	5	6. 4. 6.	1. 4.10.	2. 5. 0.	1.14.11.
Vatsker	40	109.16. 0.	2.14.10.	26. 2. 0.	2. 7. 9.

Friday 3 Oct[r]

Went to Coll Farm House and went over the buildings with John Sheil pointing out to him what work is still to do — Met the tenants of Nether Coll who in general are very poor tho' a few among them are very comfortable, the greater number pay their rents by working at the Castle grounds and about Stornoway — A few are engaged in the fishing — Met the people of the Aird of Tong who are among the most Comfortable tenants in the Lews and pay their rents well, there are four young widows in this township who lost their husbands at Wick in 1848 they still keep the Crofts occupied by their Husbands and pay their rents most regularly — I could not but express my approbation of their Conduct before the other people of the township — Met the people of Druim Tong the greater part of whom pay pritty well, this is principally a Harris settlement they came here about 25 years ago The people of this district are preparing to begin the Haddock fishing this season, which I hope may pay well — Rigg has a very poor Crop this year being all on new land — This days work appears as follows —

	No of Tenants	Total Rent	Avge Rent	Collection	Avge Arrears
Nether Coll	48	£129.13.	£2. 9.10.	£19.10.	£2. 7.10.
Aird of Tong	22	61. 5	2.15. 8.	33.17. 6.	1.10.10.
Druim Tong	18	40.19. 6.	2. 5. 6.	17. 7. 0.	2.14. 0.

Addressed each township same as yesterday & Settled several disputed [*sic*] between the people and at home at 11 P.M.

Saturday 4

At office going over pay bills for Farm Work at Holm & Sand^k Hill which I fear will exceed what can be made of the produce which is small on the new land — Examining paybills for Workmen at Castle pointing jobbing etc — gave order for payment of same — Meeting parties & writing letters — Went to Castle to see Sir James accompanied him to Stables and saw where thrashing mill was to be placed, Sir James wished a whin brusing & cutting machine to be added which we will endeavour to arrange — Spoke about making stable accommodation for Farm Horses in end of Granery etc Went to Gas Work and was engaged there for several Hours examining Wilsons a/cs by which examination I find he is short about £16 — Installed new manager who is to begin operations on Monday — Returned to office to write letters etc

Monday 6

At office writing letters for Packet Had meeting with Mr Milbank & Mr Hutchinson — With Mr Gair regarding Steamer a/cs and paid him freights for "Islay" — Went to Castle to see Sir James — Met Mr Ritchie and McLennan the Miller and had consultation about whin machine — Returned to office and arranged various matters — Went to Holm and walked over that farm & part of Sand^k Hill with Mr Houston Sn^r with the view of getting an offer from him, but did not succeed in getting him to terms his ideas not being above one half of what I could expect — I consider both should bring a rent of £200 tho' they might be let at less for the first few years — There is a good crop of potatoes turnips at Holm I estimate about 500 barrels of the former which should sell @ 3/- to 4/- per barrel. The Flax Crop is stacked & no prospect of getting it sold so much for Mr Bowies golden dreams — There are about 120 head of Cattle at Holm 50 to 60 of which are stots to be sent by next Steamer to South Hill, some will be sold fat in Stornoway and some kept on the farm all winter — The greater part of the crop of Holm & Sand Hill is secured — The crop of the latter is rather poor particularly the turnip being a first crop on new land —

Tuesday 7 Oct^r

At office writing letters among others to Rev^d Mr McRae Ness with state of arrears in his Parish & telling him that if the people did not pay their rents they could not expect to be continued in possession of land. Called on Mr Munro about Glebe Case who advised me not to write Mr McRae — About Mr John Mackenzies Charter, Alex^r Mackenzies a/cs etc Met the Rev^d Mr McRae who explained that the ground he inten[d]ed to improve was what was designed as a grass Glebe in 1807 [*sic*] that the boundaries were distinctly mentioned in the Presbytery records and the marks still be be seen on the ground — Had meeting with Mr D Mackenzie and Alex Mackenzie regarding settlement of the a/c of the latter for work done during Mr Scobies management Mr D Mackenzie brings out a balance of £17 against him — A Mackenzie Started with denying Mr Scobies meal & timber account which he addmitted as correct after seeing his orders except a few bolls of meal given by Mr Fairbairn which Mr F. is prepared to prove — Some further information is required on both sides and another meeting fixed for Monday next, the balance in dispute is now small and it will be well to give in in some doubtful points to obtain a discharge in full — Attended meeting of Water Co^y and instaled James Anderson as manager of these Works — Wrote particular instructions for his guidance & hope the Works will go on in a more satisfactory manner under his charge — Went to Castle to see Sir James accompanied him to Stable tried Gas Stove — Arranged various matters with Mr Howitt — Returned to office etc

Wednesday 8 Oct^r

At office all day settling a/cs with John Morison — John McFarquhar for Smith work for Home, Holm and Sand^k Farms which are very extravagant made deductions & paid same — McFarquhar having declined to Contract for the Farm Work have engaged with D McDonald @ 50/- per annum for each horse — shewing, repairing ploughs carts etc included in that sum — Settled with Donald & Ken McLeod for work done by them. Writing letter for Steamer till 12 o'clo[c]k

Thursday 9 Oct^r

At Sandwick met the people of New Market, there is but one rent due by some of them there, but their arrears at Bayhead is brought to their debit, they paid little or nothing and as they had to remove build new houses etc they must get a little indulgence — Met the people of Laxdale & Guirshader some of whom are good payers and others very bad, one old man Duncan Mackenzie who has a good House & a horse and cart is £23.10 in arrear and only paid Sir James 1/4 since he purchased the Estate Another man Rod^k Morison near Laxdale Bridge is £18.12.8. in arrear he has also a horse & cart both these people should be ejected they have got summonses of removal, there are several widows who are much in arrear of rent but for them there may be some excuse — Met the people of Coulregrean & Garyscore who pay pritty well — This days work appears as follows

New Market	15	9.15. 0.	0.13. 0.	1. 7. 2.	3. 0. 3.
New Valley	9	8. 1. 9.	17.11.	0. 0. 0.	3.15. 8.
Laxdale & Lane					
River	19	30. 6. 1.	1.11.10.	2.12. 6.	3. 3. 8.
Coulregrean	14	27. 2. 0.	1.18. 8.	4. 2. 0.	1.19. 7.
Garyscore	4	12. 0. 0.	3. 0. 0.	- - -	1. 0. 8.

Went to office and wrote letters for Steamer, saw Cattle shipped for Southhill arranged with John Mackenzie for disposal of same & with Mr Cameron about proceeding to Falkirk —

Friday 10 Oct[r]

At Sandwick met a few of the people of Lower Sandwick, the greater part of whom did not even shew face tho' three years in arrear of rent — Their farm I have no doubt is over rented particularly as the whole of their pasture ground was taken off and added to Stoneyfield, they are almost all served with notices of removal and those who do not shew any desire to pay must be deprived of land, and what remains of the farm may be divided among those who pay at a reduced rent — Went over the accounts of the people of Sand[k] Hill, they were much in arrear last year, but the greater part of them have paid up except some old people who are on the Poors Roll — Met the people of Holm who on the whole pay well, that farm is also much over rented almost the whole of its pasture land being taken off and added to Upper Holm & Stoneyfield — This days work appears as follows

Widows Row	7	3. 9. 5.	0. 9.11.	3. 0. 1.	1. 8. 7.
Lower Sandk	25	40.13. 1.	1.12. 6.	3.16. 2.	5. 3. 8.
Sandk Hill	59	44. 3. 0.	0.15. 0.	4. 4. 0.	18. 0.
Holm	11	35. 0. 0.	3. 3. 7.	12.13. 6.	3.10. 9.

Arranged with Mr J. R. M[c]Lean to send his vessel the Duchess to take on board the kelp on the west side between Galson and Shawbost which is such a bad Coast that it is ill to get a vessel at any rate of freight to undertake it A vessel of D. M[c]Leans made the atempt but was driven off & took in her cargo at Loch Roag — the rate of freight agreed on to Glasgow is 15/- per ton long weight —

Saturday 11 Oct[r]

Went to office and was engaged writing letters, going over a/cs of work done on Goathill farm with Mr Ritchie — Called on Mr. Munro regarding Glebe case, Kennedys & Co[ys] reference & revised same, Summoning parties in arrear, Mr Scobies a/cs etc etc Wrote letters to Gerrie & A. M[c]Leod to employ people of Ballallan & Laxay to form Branch Road to Valtos with statute labour — Called at Castle to see Sir James — Went to Stables — Arranged various matters with Mr Howitt — Returned to office, wrote letters, one to Mr. Finlayson Lochs about arrears of Carloway district telling him that that district of his parish must be cleared if the people did not pay their rents — settled a/cs with McMillans for fencing — Went to Gas Works and arranged with manager to make coke for Castle etc

Monday 13 Oct^r

Went to home Farm and remained there during the forenoon getting the Oats still on the field put into heaps — Bowie should have been more active in securing the crop in the earlier part of the Season — Went to office and met Mr Munro settled Eliots account with him for Work done during Mr Scobie's management amounting to £59.13.3.. Met Mr D MacKenzie & Alex McKenzie regarding the a/c of the latter, but there being some evidence awanting delayed settlement till next week — met Gerrie McCallum and McMillan & settled a/cs with them Wrote letters, went to Castle to see Sir James, Left for Galson at 4 o'clock accompanied by Mr Donald Matheson —

Tuesday 14 Oct^r

Left Galson at 10 A.M. for Borve where I remained all day, met the people of North Galson Upper Shader & Lower Shader and took Cattle and a few pounds of Cash from them — Went over their several accounts. Their payments etc are as follows

	No. of Ten.	Total Rent	Avge Rent	Payt	Arrears
N Galson	59	£157.16. 8.	£2.13. 6.	£41.19/-	£5. 8. 5.
Upr Shader	27	120. 6.-	4. 9. -.	23.17.1	8.11. 1.
Lowr Shader	33	100. 3.	3. -. 8.	9.2/-	6. 2. 5.
Ballintroushal	17	49.16.	2.18/-	—	5. 3. 1.

The greater number of the N Galson tenants do their best to pay rents — There is an Angus Graham who built a good house there but has never paid any rent, nor paid for some materials given him to assist in building his house, he must be removed if he does not pay — Mr McPherson will take his Croft & House for a Shepherd and pay the rent — The people of Shaders are yearly falling more into arrear of rent, they shew no wish to pay & it would seem as if a combination existed amongst them not to pay the landlord as many of them are in possession of a good Stock of Sheep & Cattle tho' others have few or none — 10 Families from Lower Shader emigrated and 2 from Upper & many of the rest are preparing to follow & have no desire to pay rents — The people on the new land seem to be doing well and are more anxious to pay their rents — They have formed a portion of the Ness Road, and completed some of the drainage works, which when measured and settled for will nearly pay their rents — Sent Donald Mackenzie, Dalbeg (who is acting for his son) to the Shaders & Borves to warn them to attend tomorrow with Cash or Cattle — Returned to Galson at 9 P.M. —

Wednesday 15

The weather being very bad could not cross Borve River, remained at Galson till 3 P.M. Went to Borve School House and there went over the a/cs of each tenant in Melbost, Mid & Five Penny Borve, and having done so addressed the people on the subject of their not paying rents, that in consiquence of their dishonesty and laziness they must be deprived of their holdings & if they did not shew a greater willingness to pay a change must be made at next term — As the weather was so bad today they did not bring forward Cattle but determined on waiting tomorrow and ordered them to meet me here at 10 o'clock Returned to Galson at 10 P.M.

Thursday 16

Went to Borve and after having sent three messengers to Five Penny Borve to attend with Cattle or Money to pay their rents and seeing that but few appeared, went to the sea shore where their Cattle were pasturing accompanied by Mr McPherson Galson, Mr A McIver & Dalbeg Collected their Cattle and horses and drove them to the Road, but before we got them so far the greater number were secured in their houses — Tho' no one could be seen when they were sent for, men, women & children now appeared in all directions some driving off a cow, some running away with a Horse etc etc Being overpowered by numbers we succeeded in taking but few of their Cattle, and the greater number of those we did get we had to let go as we could not ascertain the owners names, some of whom very coolly offered & paid money for their Cattle tho' they formerly denied having any — The people of this township have a good Stock of Sheep and Cattle and have always had good Crops, there is no doubt but the greater number of them could pay if they pleased The part of Mid Borve formerly held by Robt Murray is now occupied by 8 families from Reef who own a Wick boat & nets and can pay their rents — They seem quite satisfied with the change they have made — The other tenants of Mid Borve are the most destitute in the parish and are all old men, 2 families Emigrated from this township — The people of Melbost Borve are better off than their neighbours of Mid Borve but have not such a good stock as those of Five Penny — [no figure shown] Families Emigrated from this township — Their Accounts & Collection stands thus

	No. of Ten^ts	Tot Rent	Avge Rent	Coll^ion	Avge Arrears
Five Penny Borve	35	£118	£3.17.	£48.17/-	£6. 4. 7.
Mid Borve Uig men	8	25	3. 2. 6.	[sum erased]	1. 2. 3.
Mid Borve	8	27	3. 7. 6.	24.15/	5.18. 1.
Melbost Borve	21	55. 6.	2.12. 8.	10.12/-	5. -. 6.

Should these farms be cleared Galson Farm might be extended to Borve River & include Mid & Melbost Borve which would give it a good run for sheep —Between the River of Borve & the River of Shader would make another good sheep farm, and the School House of Borve might be converted into a farm House If the price of black Cattle does not rise these people cannot pay rent and the sooner they are sent off the less the loss by them — Counted over the Cattle 70 in number and put them under charge of herds — Called at the Manse of Barvas & dined got home at 12 P.M.

Friday 17

Going over a/cs, writing letters, and examining rentals at office till 4 P.M. — Went to the Castle to see Sir James, had talk on various matters— Sir James wishes to engage Campbell the Forister for one year from Martinmas next @ £42 per annum to live at the Cottage built for the piper & to have grass for two cows and a patch of land — Arranged various matters with Howitt & Bowie Settled a/cs with Fraser painter, Gas Co^y etc etc —

Saturday 18th

Went to Holm Farm and selected the Cattle to be sold today, those to be sent to the South by next steamer & those to be wintered on the farm, gave directions to McIntosh on various subjects — Proceeded to Guirshader and went over the Cattle there, took out of them those that will sell, Went to Park at E. Chapel & inspected the Cattle there — Went to office and wrote letter of engagement for Campbell the Forester, met various parties — Called on Mr Munro & Sheriff McDonald about Court House — Attended sale of Cattle sold 33 at an average price of £2.4/- being rather more than what they would sell for at Falkirk without being at the expence of sending them there — Returned to the office and made out Cattle lists, settled with herds, settled a/cs with various parties etc etc

Monday 20

Went to office and was engaged meeting parties, masters of vessels about kelp, writing statement for Advertiser regarding Emigrants — Attended meeting of Parochial Board and was detained there for five hours —Went to Court Room with the Sheriff & Mr Munro to see alterations of seating required by these gentlemen — Revised Minute of Reference in Kennedys business — Went to Castle to see Sir James returned to office and wrote letters for Packet, arranged various matters and left for Callanish at 9 P.M. arrived there at 12 —

Tuesday

At Callanish all day meeting with people from the Carloway district. Several cows were offered for rent but were refused as they were of such inferior quality that they would not sell at market — Went over the a/cs of the Callanish tenants and arranged with Mr J. McDonald to store the kelp still in his district at Carloway — etc

Wednesday 22

Settling with the people of Braiscalate Callanish & Garynahine for kelp. Arranged with Mr A McIver to proceed to Barnera to collect rents as I had to return to Stornoway to sort and arrange Cattle for shipping per Steamer — George McLeod says he is to give up the Inn of Callanish at the term of Whitsunday next — Proceeded to Guirshader and arranged the Cattle into three lots 55 cows and 7 horses for Market, 14 old cows for Lodge farm and 12 young ones for Holm, sold eight — Went over farm with Bowie & pushed him about securing his Crop — Went over Cattle from Holm Farm but found none fit for Market, sent 8 to Lodge farm. Went to office and wrote letters for Packet, arranged with John MacKenzie to proceed to Doune with Cattle, etc etc

Thursday 23

Went to office and was engaged settling with Mr Cameron for Cattle sold at Falkirk, with Mr McAulay Linshader for rents, let to him what is not required of the turnip on the meadow — Went over monthly a/cs and settled same — Paid Dr Millar his yearly salary — Arranged with Mr W^m McKay for his brothers a/cs — Called on Mr Munro but did not find him at home — Went to Castle and saw dial fixed by Sarg^t Barlow — Sir James pointed out site of Coal Cellar which he wishes to be cut out of rock, consulted him on various subjects — Returned to office and prepared Specification for Bridge in Harris — etc etc

Friday 24

Went to Mr Ken Morrisons Feu to settle disputed boundary — Had meeting with Rev^d Mr McGrigor & called on Mr Munro to consult him about Police Rogue Money etc Settled with Dr Millar — Called at Castle to see Sir James — Went to Guirshader and arranged line of fence with Mr Ritchie & Mr

Houston, to shut up part of Barvas Street — Went over Roads made & repairing by Houston & Co[y] — Went to Guirshader to see Houses built & building for poor people removing from Bayhead — Saw Bowie regarding securing his Crop — Returned to office to write letters for the Packet etc

Saturday 25

At office meeting parties Mr D Mackenzie & Alex Mackenzie regarding the settlement of the latters a/c but separated again without coming to a settlement — Donald Mackenzie regarding his a/c for cleaning streets — He has nothing to get being paid more than he was entitled to, not having repaired & cleaned the streets according to Specification. Sir James called at office & had some talk about Uig Glebe etc. Settled with Collector of poor for balance of Stornoway Parish rates — Had meeting with Mr Munro, on various subjects — Writing letters etc etc

Monday 27 Oct[r]

Went to office met Mess[rs] Houston and arranged to go over land which they wish drained, Sand[k] Hill etc — Granted order for payment of workmen at Castle & grounds, writing letters and meeting parties — Attended meeting of Parochial Board and was detained there till 1/2 past 4 — Returned to the office and wrote Mr Munro on various subjects etc

Tuesday 28 Oct[r]

At office writing paper on Emigration. Attended a J.P. Court — Went to Distillery to see men paid — Went over workshops stables etc — Called at Castle to see Sir James — Went over Esplanade House with John Mackenzie & his wife and put it under their charge to keep on fires etc Returned to office arranged with Bowie to clean streets & remove the scrapings to the grounds for manure — Settled with John Smith for his Contracts for Uig and Loch Morskill Road

Wednesday 29 Oct[r]

Went to Melbost and saw land to be drained by Mr Houston, he offers to drain 9 acres of meadow at his own expence if the Proprietor will give tiles & soles which may be granted — there will still remain 21 acres of the low carse land to drain which the tenant offers to do at £3 per acre & pay interest on the outlay — He will lay out the money if the amount is sustained in his rent — If this were done Melbost would be a complete & well improved farm Walked over each field of Sandwick Hill to ascertain the quality of moss land in each, accompanied by Mr Houston — Saw the Marches proposed for Holm and fixed to meet in the evening Went to Stornoway & attended a meeting of the Water Co[y] — Went to the office and wrote letters Met various parties & got contents of Holm & Sand Hill. Engaged at home with

Mr Houston till 2 A.M. endeavouring to arrange with him a rent for these farms — My Idea was that if Sand^k Hill were once laid down is [sic] should let at nearly £150 being 153 acres, but it will take 5 or 6 years before the land could be in such order as yield that rent, and there is a considerable portion of it deep moss that will never give more than 10/- per acre, — Seeing that a large outlay is still required each year to put the land in heart and that it would be desirable to let it and that Houston if he took it and Holm would not require any steading at Sand^k Hill I reduced my estimate to £100 — and £50 for Holm — He first offered only £100 for both farms — After valuing each field in Sand^k Hill he increased his offer to about £90 but would give no more than £32 for Holm or £122 for both — so we seperated. I hope he may yet come up tho' he says he is determined not to give another penny —

Thursday 30

At office till 3 O clock writing letters for Steamer, remitted several a/cs — Accompanied Sir James to Guirshader, saw Houses & land of new settlers there returned by Mary Bank Went to office and arranged various matters — Instructed Mr Ritchie to go to Tong to make Survey of Glebe — got Donald McLeod an old man to accompany him to shew Marches etc

Friday 31 Oct^r

Went to Laxdale & Guirshader and let the part of these places north of the new dike to those of the former tenants who paid their rents, the indurance of their lease to be 15 years if they pay their rents & improve their crofts — Nearly a third of the former tenants have been deprived of land and their lots are still vaccant, if they pay before Martinmas they may be continued — Went to the Court House and sat in judgement on two criminal cases one of theft — Jane McLean to which she pleaded guilty, sentenced her to 20 days imprisonment — The other for assault by John McLean to which he pleaded guilty, sentenced him to pay a fine of 20/- or six days imprisonment — Went to the office, wrote letters settled a/cs — Met parties — Went to Tong and walked over the Marches of the Grass Glebe as pointed out by Donald McLeod an old man from the Aird of Tong, a few of the old Marks can be traced but not sufficient to delineate the Marches, McLeod however points out the direction of the March which answers the description of the designation — Walked over the Marches of the arable glebe, the Minister occupied more than 8 Scotch acres, and that quantity is in no way defined. Mr Ritchie is now engaged making a survey of the whole —
The additional arable land as stated by the old man McLeod was given to the Minister (Mr Cameron) by Mr Adam in exchange for a shealing and the fence seperating that ground from the glebe was at the same time removed — McLeod pointed out the original March of the arable glebe which Mr Ritchie will lay down on his plan —

...ntals of the farms we
...over today —

Sunday 7 Nov. 1837
... to the Free Church School
... at Crossbost, and there
the people of the farms
...erbost, Crossbost, Ranish
... finished and had ad-
...ressed them on the terms
...ase being 15 years from
...sunday first, the regular
...rent of rents being the first
...ition, improving their Crofts
...es the second, keeping their
...ren at School, paying Statute
...r for the third proceedi...
... Luerbost to 57 tenants
... average rent of £2.13/-
...ing the total rental of
...arm £151-15/ An increase
... over the old rent — Sum...

Saturday 1 Nov[r]

Went to the office and went over last months a/cs — Had meeting with Mr Munro on various subjects — Signed several papers for Sheriff Had meeting with Mr Nisbits regarding his a/c — Went to Castle & consulted with Sir James on various matters — Mrs Perceval pointed out site of proposed mound to shut office buildings & Bayhead from the view of the Castle & wishes a plan & estimate to be prepared — Accompanied Sir James in making a minute inspection of the ground lying between the Creed approach and the MaryBank approach with the view of enclosing the portion on which the planting does not thrive, to be improved as pasture by burning, sheep draining, and top dressing or soiling — Went to Square to what is doing in workships [sic] several of the joiners should be paid off — Went to office, meet parties & arranged matters etc

Monday 3 Nov[r]

At office going over monthly accounts, meeting with Mr Munro on various business — Capt[n] Burnaby Mr Hutchinson etc etc Went to Castle to see Sir James — arranged with Kenneth M[c]Leod to form mound as marked out above having [sic] to be paid £15 for the work, but if done in a satisfactory manner he is to get £20 — Arranged various matters with Mr Howitt — Returned to office and met Alexander & Rigg — Settled accounts with Mr Nisbit — Wrote to fish Curers with lists of rents promised to be paid by them for Fishermen. Wrote to Uig Ground Officer fixing meetings for next week & to the Lochs G. Officer for meetings this week — Wrote letters to several parties —

Tuesday 4 Nov[r]

At office meeting parties the Banker, Mr Munro, Mr J MacKenzie, Sloain etc Writing letters — Went to Castle to Call for Sir James — Left for Lochs — Walked over the farm of Laxay — Saw each lot in the Township with a view to fix the rents — Proceeded to Val[t]os and remained there all night

Wednesday 5 Nov[r]

Went to Laxay and let the crofts of that Township 31 in number at an average rent of £2.15/- The Total rent being £85.7/- an increase of £5.7 over the old rent — This is a good farm and has a considerable extent of outrun which enable the people to keep a good stock of cattle & sheep and is still a cheap farm. There are several very respectable tenants in this township, some who were in arrear of rent did not get land and others were put on bad lots

Proceeded to Koes and having walked over the crofts let the same to those who had paid their rents, and left others vaccant to be given the parties who should first pay up their arrears — This farm has been over rented, the crofts are very poor, tho' the moor attached is good — There are now 14 crofts paying a rent of £42.14 being £7.6 less than the former rent — I addressed the people of these townships and explained to them the conditions of Let to be 15 years from Whitsunday next, while they paid their rents regularly, improved their Crofts, sent their children to school etc etc — Dined at the Manse and walked to Soval where I wrote letters for the Steamer to Sir James etc

Thursday 6 Nov[r]

Walked over the different lots in the Township of Luerbost & examined the same with the view of fixing the rents — This farm seems under rented and much land can be improved — Walked over each lot in the Township of Crossbost, which are very small less than three acres, but the people being all fishermen they do not so much depend on the produce of their Crofts — They are among the best payers on the Estate — Their pasture is much overstocked by Cattle there being not a blade of grass to be seen — The present rent £60 is the full value of the farm — Walked over the crofts in the township of Raenish which are considerable in extent but the greater part is hill & rock — It is the roughest ground I ever saw cultivated — The Situation is roma[n]tic situated between Loch Erisort & Loch Grimishader. This farm is much over rented & there are several poor people in it — Crossed to Grimishader and walked over the crofts of that farm and Kean Hurnivick the land of which is rather rough but can be much improved and as there is good & extensive grazing they can pay a small increase of rent — Returned to Soval & arrived at 9 P.M. — Arranged the rentals of the farms we went over today —

Friday 7 Nov[r] 1851

Went to the Free Church School House at Crossbost, and there met the people of the Farms of Luerbost, Crossbost, Raenish & Grimishader and having addressed them on the terms of Lease being 15 years from Whitsunday first, the regular payment of rents being the first Condition, improving their Crofts & Houses the second, keeping their children at School, paying statute Labour etc etc the third, proceeded to Let Luerbost to 57 tenants at an average rent of £2.13/- making the total rental of the farm £151.15/- an increase £16.16/- over the old rent — This farm is still moderately rented but it is over peopled — If they are industrious they can add considerably to the arable land — Let Crossbost to 28 tenants at an average rent of of £2.4/- The total rent being as before £60 —

Let the farms of Raenish to 40 tenants at an average rent of £2.18 being a total rent of £116.9 or £14.11/- less than formerly paid — There were several people who formerly held land in this township now deprived of it as they did not pay their rents — Let Grimishader and Kean Hurnivick to 14 tenants at an average rent of £2.17 making a total of £40.2/ being an increase of £5.2/- This farm is still more moderately rented than Raenish — Dined at the School House and returned to Soval at 12 P.M. The people seem generally well pleased with the days proceedings — Mr Cameron deserves much merit for the way in which he has divided the land in these townships giving the people facilities of improving their Crofts which they did not formerly enjoy. And Mr McLeod for his complete knowledge of the peoples character means etc did the other ground officers take such an interest in seeing that the rents were paid & possess so much local knowledge as Mr McLeod the factors labours would be more successful and less arduous —

Saturday 8 Nov^r

At Soval all day receiving rents and settling disputes among the people — Got home at 9 P.M. —

Monday 10

Went to the Office, met parties — Went to the Castle to call for Sir James, saw work doing at mound — Inspected workshops etc   Called on Mr Munro — Attended meeting of Parochial Board & was detained there for some time. Returned to office and arranged various matters was obliged to go home rather unwell —

Tuesday 11

At office going over corrispondence regarding Glebe Case & objections to drainage loan — Amending same with Mr Munro — Meeting Sir James Mr D L MacKenzie etc — Settled Steamer a/cs etc with Mr Gair. Wrote letters for Packet — Settled various a/cs — Left for Callanish at 7 P.M.

Wednesday 12

Left Callanish at 10 P.M.[*sic*] Called at Linshader but did not find Mr McAulay at home — Called at the Sound of Barnera and took in Mr Ken Stewart & John McDonald Ground Officer — After arriving at Kean Langavate proceeded to the March between Tumisgary and Valtos where we met the Rev^d Mr Watson and the Tenants of Valtos — The disputed ground at this point Mr Watson admitted was not worth three shillings per annum — Kenneth Stewart pointed out the old March between both farms, and the new March or that fixed by Mr Alex Stewart Factor of Lews in 1826. — The old March goes by an old dyke to the East of Forsnaval, the new March is drawn in a direct line from the top of that hill to a red scar on the South side of Glen Valtos, giving a small portion of the pasture of Tumisgary to Valtos — Tumisgary at the time of the alteration was occupied by Small tenants who ultimately agreed with their neighbours about this boundary tho' at first they had some disputes — When George Mitchell entered the farms of Tumisgary and Erista in 1836 Kenneth Stewart then ground officer was sent to point out the boundaries to him he not knowing that the Factor had altered the March at this point pointed out the old boundary to Mitchell — He did not at this time walk over the other Marches of the farm but merely discribed them — The Valtos tenants all along disputed this boundary with Mitchell, but being of little value to either party it never was brought to a settlement farther than that Mr Knox referring to this particular boundary told Mr Mitchell to keep possession of what he had got — We proceeded to the top of Forsnaval where Mr Watson for the first time told me that the Marches he now claimed were those held by the PO. Mr Munro and the old tenants of Tumisgary & Erista which included the Middle Hills and Kean Reasort — I replied that these Marches he would never be put in possession of, that the farm of Tumisgary was only let to him as held by his predecessor George Mitchell — We arranged to meet at the School House in the evening to take evidence but some of the people having come to settle rents did not sent for Mr Watson —

Thursday 13th

Sent notice to Mr Watson that I intended to take evidence on his Marches and would be glad that he would attend — Mr Watson at once appeared and asked me before going farther to decide the March between him and Valtos which I had seen yesterday but which I declined to do till I had heard the whole evidence. He then stated that if I would not decide this point he would not wait, that he was fully determined to claim the old Marches held by Mr Munro and the tenants of Tumisgary and that he would hear of none else, on which he walked away notwithstanding my request that he should wait to hear the evidence — Mr Cameron took down the Evidence of Kenneth Stewart the late Ground Officer & George Mitchell the former tenant describing the Marches as possessed by the latter, and it was determined to perambulate these Marches tomorrow so far as not seen yesterday — Wrote

Mr Watson of my intention that he might have an opportunity of accompanying us which he said he would Met the people of Braenish Islivick, Carnish, Mangersta, Croulista, Valtos & Kneep — Got some small sums of money and gave notice of the parties in each farm which are deprived of land for not paying rent — Told the people of Carnish & Kneep who shew no willingness to pay that the whole of these farms must be cleared at next term — Received four letter[s] from Mr. Watson which I answered in one —

Friday 14th

Inspected the offices now building at Uig Manse — Paid instal[e]ment to Contractor — Met the people of Aird Uig regarding their rents & got some small sums from them — Wrote Mr Watson in answer to four letters received from him this morning — Started for the perambulation of the Marches of Tumisgary farm accompanied by Mr Cameron George Mitchell Ken Stewart, James McRae for Mr Watson John McRae Reef James Mackenzie Edreroel and Neil McKay an old tenant of Tumisgary — We proceeded along the March between Edreroel & Tumisgary viz the River Awin n' Orse Loch Lacksavat and Loch Suanavat thence up Awin Cromagh n' tilleugh to Aven na Nien where it leaves the Edreroel March and crosses a ridge near Esvadhu to a mark on the West Bank of Loch Grounavate which it crosses in an easterly direction to the foot of Deirisben thence in a northerly direction on a track by the eastern shoulder of Suanaval and from that point by Arri Herepie to Glen Val[t]os — These boundaries were those fixed by Mr Stewart factor of Lews in 1827 and occupied thereafter by the tenants of Tumisgary and Erista — They claimed no more & restricted their stock to these boundaries — Mitchell got possession of the farm according to these boundaries and never claimed more hence the present tenant Mr Watson cannot extend his claims beyond what his predecessor occupied — The whole of the parties agreed to the above described boundary — Walked to Carishader thence took boat to the Free Church Manse where I dined — Proceeded to Callanish where I arrived at 12 P.M. —

Saturday 15 Nov^r

Arranged various matters at Callanish Met Mr McAulay Linshader about John McRae's reference – Also as to land at Balligloum which he wishes to take — Proceeded to Stornoway Called at Castle to see Sir James — saw work done at mound went over workshops etc Proceeded to office entered cash received at Uig & read letters which arrived in my absence etc etc

Monday 17

Went to office and arranged various matters — Called on Mr Munro regarding Tong & Uig Glebes & Watsons disputed Marches, Urquharts a/c etc Met Sir James there & conversed with him on these points — Settled with Thomas Clark for Cattle sold at former sale — and attended another sale of inferior Cattle, being those that could not be sent to Market they sold at an average of £1-15/-. Exposed some of the old Bulls but did not sell but one the price offered being too low — Returned to office & wrote Mr Munro regarding Smith & McLays a/c Going over account of money laid out in Drainage improvements — Sorting papers etc

Tuesday 18

At office going over accounts of drainage works with Mr McDonald and accounts for Completing works still to pay on west side — Met Mr Norman McIver regarding appropriating balance of assessment still in Bank to executing some small repairs required on the Manse & offices — Meeting Mr M.McLeod & John McKay — The Banker on various matters— Wrote letter to the Rev^d Mr McRae about survey of his glebe — Compared copies of corrispondence & sent same to Sir James — Called on Mr Munro & shewed him my letter which he revised etc etc—

Wednesday 19

At Office writing letters & meeting parties Went to Castle to Call for Sir James as to sale of House to Mrs Watt etc. Went to workshops to see what was doing — Returned to office was engaged with Mr Munro Mr Callender Mr McGrigor & the Gardiner — Writing letters for the Steamer — Engaged till 11 P.M. with Mr Callender settling accounts between Mr Scobie Mr McAulay Linshader etc etc

Thursday 20th

Went to office wrote letter Met Mr Callender — Mr McLeod Valtos — Went to Garrabost and went over the accounts of the tenants of Upper & Lower Bayble, Knock, Swordale & Garrabost — Deprived 12 tenants of land in Lower Bayble 5 in Swordale and 9 in Garrabost — If they pay up their arrears within a month they are to be taken on again — Got home at 8 P.M.

Friday 21

Had meeting with McPherson Galson about Tussoc Grass and land he wants drained — With Kenneth Stewart Hacalate who wishes to give up his Farm and go to America if he can get what will carry him there after paying his debts — Went to Castle to Call on Sir James regarding Ministers letters, sale of House to Mrs Watt etc — Went to Sheshader accompanied by Mr Cameron and walked over the Crofts of that Township with the view to reducing the rent — Considered it over rented and lowered it to £60 being the old rent before it was relotted, with interest on the ring fence & improvements   This seemed to give great satisfaction tho I consider the place still high enough — Went to Garabost and went over the accounts of the tenants of Port Naguran, Port Vollar, Aird, Sheshader and Suilishader — Deprived three tenants of land at Port Vollar 4 at Aird 5 at Sheshader & 2 at Shuilishader — Got £58 at this Collection — Returned home at 10 P.M.

Saturday 22

At office writing letters, Met Mr Callender — Went to Slip to see about repairs of Road — Pointed out to Mr Gerrie how same was to be done — Going over Emigrants letters — Circulars regarding Emigrants. Called at Castle to see Sir James who pointed out situation of Embankment which he wishes to be put up etc — Met Mr Callender & D Mackenzie and went over various unsettled a/cs and claims with them — Writing Reports on Watsons Marches with Mr Cameron etc —

Monday 24

At office writing letters — Filling up Tax Returns — Meeting parties Went to Melbost to attend Mrs Hustons interment — Accompanied Sir James from Sand^k to Bayhead — Returned to office met Kenneth Stewart etc Received letters by Packet wrote letters

Thursday 25

Went to office examined plan of Glebe — arranged various matters Went over rent Collections — Went to Castle with Mr Ritchie Sir James & Lady Matheson pointed out alteration of Road & site of mound — Returned to office had meeting with Mr Munro regarding Glebe Case & Watsons Marches — The Rev^d Mr McRae who paid his rent — Engaged during the remaining part of the day with Mr Callender & D McKenzie, meeting with Lattas representatives, Rod^k McKenzie and Alex McKenzie adjusting their a/cs during Mr Scobies management —

Wednesday 26

Called on Mr Munro and went to office   Met Sir James Mr Callender & Mr Munro — going over a/cs — Met Rev^d Mr Leid & had talk on Glebe matters — Attended Interment — Went to Mr Munros office & revised Kennedys reference — Was engaged with Mr Callender at Mr Scobies a/cs   Settled Lattas a/cs — Mr Rod^k Mackenzie's except a few small matters — Writing letters for Steamer — At plans of Embankment & alteration of road etc

Thursday 27

Inspected draining doing at Sand^k pointed out alteration of gate & drain to mason at English Chapel — At office meeting Mr Callender, arranging a/cs with Mr Morison — Meeting Rev^d Mr Watson regarding his Marches but came to no terms — I offered to refer the matters in dispute to the Sheriff or Fiscal which he refused   Went with Mr C to consult Mr Munro, met Sir James explained the matter to him — Arranged with John Mackenzie as to value of sheds in Market place — Consulted Sir James as to K Stewarts arrears, he will forgive one half if he emigrates   Wrote Stewart — Engaged with Mr Callender at Mr Scobies a/cs   Meeting Mr Nicolson etc — Writing parties etc

Friday 28

Went to the office and examined monthly a/cs, past orders for same — Met with Mr Callender regarding Mr Scobies a/cs   Went to Castle to Call for Sir James regarding Watsons Marches, Emigration etc — Went to Coll inspected work doing there by John Sheill — Met the people of North & South Tolsta, Back, Vatsker, Coll, Tong and Aird of Tong — Went over the a/cs of 214 tenants and saw each of them, craved for rent but only got £28 — The people of Tolsta are so far behind with the payment of their rents that I see no prospect of their ever being able to pay up — The other farms in this district are pretty well paid up and shew every wish to pay their rents — Gave notice to all the desparate characters who were summoned out last year & did not endeavour to pay that they would not be allowed to lay down a crop next Spring   Got home at 11 P.M.

Saturday 29

Went to office and read over Emigrants letters — Met Mr Callender regarding Sheild's & Christies a/cs Also Messrs Munro & Pirrie on the same subject — Settled with Brock — Arranged accounts with Mr C J Nicolson for Securities granted by him for Fishermen — Arranged accounts with the Banker for Fishermens a/cs Feu duties, Store Rents, also for a/c due him — Meeting Mr Alexander who paid part of his rent — Mr Houston, Rig — etc etc Arranged with Mr Ritchie various matters — Meeting country people, writing letters, at rental a/c etc etc

...eeting of Parochial Board
...eeting Mr. Morrison Banker
...Mr. Auly Mr. Munro Mr. Callen...
...apts. Brvmaly to writing le...
...oing over notes by Mr. C on I
...ps — do

Tuesday 9 Dec.

...led on Mr. Munro saw his Corresponde...
...the Minister — was engaged at the of...
Callender, going over various aps — Meetin...
...and officer — Went to the Bank to arrange be...
...e — Engaged with Mr. Callender & Mr. Gair...
...mer aps and Mr. Scobies Accounts & h —

Wednesday 10 De.

...t to office and arranged various matters, the...
...stle, saw Sir James & Lady Matheson about new...
...removing oldone — Returned to office and...
...s with Mr. Callender at Mr. Scobies aps — Wrote M...
...in answer to his mis-statements — Going over...
...new Garden with Mr. Ritchie — Writing letters for
    12 Rd...

Thursday 11

...office writing letters, going over and settling accou...
...ld in full with Alex Mackenzie for Roval Perline...
...Sir James about Post office & Watsons letters — A...
...ting of Water Coy regarding an aps of Mr. Nabs for we...
...presented as Chairman — Meeting with Mr. Callender...
...who referred matters in dispute to Mr. MAuly & Mr. C...
...te Clark to rescign the Post office or School — Calle...
...es — Revised Charter prepared for Mr. John Mackenzie...
...the measurements given includes John Mackenzie...
...the adjoining one — Settle d Mr B Mr C.

Monday 1 Decr 1851

Went to office, met Mr Callender, granted orders for payment of monthly accounts — Settled with various parties for salaries etc — Went to Castle to see Sir James — Returned to office & was engaged writing letters for packet meeting parties etc — S[t]arted for Ness at 8 P.M. and arrived at Swanabost at 1 A.M. — Contracted with Murdo McLeod Glen House to keep the Barvas Road in repair between the Black Water & Barvas River a distance of 9 miles for £4.10/- per annum

Tuesday 2 Dec^r

At Swanabost meeting the tenants of the different Townships in the District of Ness, almost all of whom I saw & craved for rent but with little success — Tho' the people of this district have great advantages in respect of fishing & fertile land, they are farther behind than any others who have the same advantages — Settled with labourers for finishing up drainage works — I have lost all hopes of getting the people of Eoropy Five Penny Ness & the Dells to pay up their arrears of rent — There are great complaints of Munro the Miller that he does not attend to his Mill the people being often in want of food as they cannot get their corn ground —He is a worthless fellow, neglects his business & has left his home and wife with another woman — As Wednesday is a fast day sat up till 9 A.M. of that day to get finished with the people of the district —

Wednesday 3

Slept from 9 till 12 — After arranging various matters left Ness for Galson intending to meet the people of that district but as they were all at Church delayed meeting till tomorrow —

Thursday 4

Went to Borve School Ho and after examining some of the classes — met the people of N Galson the Three Borves and two Shaders and after going over each tenant and spending 12 hours with them did not get more than 50/- There can be nothing gained in leaving the people of the Borves & Shaders in possession of land as they will not and cannot pay rent — They are the worst in every respect of all the tenants of the Lews — and there is hardly a good man among them — Gave them notice that they might look out for a change — It would be well if they could be got to emigrate in a body — Settled several disputes & returned to Galson at 12 P.M.

Friday 5 Dec[r]

Left Galson at 9 A.M. Called at Barvas Manse but did not See the Minister not being up — Left Mr A M[c]Iver at Barvas to collect rents — Proceeded to Arnold with Mr M[c]Donald and walked over the Crofts of that farm & of North & South Bragar & South Shawbost — Arnold & the Bragars contain little or no arable land and one is puzzled to know where or how the people can raise crops — notwithstanding, these people, who do not fish, pay better than the people of Ness — South Shawbost contains good arable land — Inspected the work doing at Shawbost Quay which is getting on rather slowly — Went on to Dalbeg & remained there for the night

Saturday 6 Dec[r]

Had some talk with Mr Hutchinson about the Soval shooting but his ideas of rent are rather low, his object seems to be to secure the fishing of the Black River — Went to Shawbost school House, and relet the Township of Arnold to those of the old tenants who had paid up their rents, leaving several lots vaccant to be given to those in arrear if they pay up within a month — Did the same with North & South Bragar — and received several sums of money. The people of these townships till within the last few years were the very worst in the Lews, but they are yearly improving in their appearance, morals & means — And the rising generation is rather promising — They own several large Wick boats with a stock of nets and have been fortunate at the Herring fishing — Met the people of South Shawbost but after going over their accounts refused to give them a new Let as they were so much in arrear of rent — Told them that if they did not pay up by next term they must prepare for a change — Left Shawbost at 1/2 past 9 & got home at 1 A.M.—

Monday 8 Dec[r]

Went to the office, read over letters received in my absence — Met parties — Went to Castle to see Sir James — Saw site proposed for new gardin, alteration of Road embank[t] etc — Went to Square Returned to office — Attended meeting of Parochial Board — Meeting Mr Morison Banker, Mr J M[c]Auly, Mr Munro, Mr Callender, Capt[n] Burnaby etc Writing letters, going over notes by Mr C on my a/cs etc

Tuesday 9 Dec[r]

Called on Mr Munro saw his corrispondence with the Minister — Was engaged at the office with Mr Callender, going over various a/cs — Meeting Uig Ground Officer — Went to the Bank to arrange business there — Engaged with Mr Callender & Mr Gair at Steamer a/cs and Mr Scobies accounts etc etc —

Wednesday 10 Dec^r

Went to office and arranged various matters there Went to Castle, Saw Sir James & Lady Matheson about new Gardin and removing old one — Returned to office and was engaged with Mr Callender at Mr Scobies a/cs — Wrote Mr Watson Uig in answer to his mis-statements — Going over Estimate of New Gardin with Mr Ritchie — Writing letters for Steamer till 12 P M

Thursday 11

At office writing letters, going over and settling accounts — Settled in full with Alex Mackenzie for Soval & Aline Stables.   Saw Sir James about Post Office & Watsons letters — Attended meeting of Water Co^y regarding an a/c of McNabs for which I am prosicuted as Chairman — Meeting with Mr Callander & McRae Arinish who referred matters in dispute to Mr McAulay & Mr Cameron Wrote Clark to resign the post office or School. Called on Mr Munro — Revised charter prepared for Mr John Mackenzie but find the measurements given include John Mackenzies Town feu the adjoining one — Settled with Mr Gerrie for his son W^{ms} a/c against Mr Scobie

Friday 12

At office all day writing letters to Tacksmen in arrear of rent to pay up — Assisting Mr Callender with Mr Scobies a/c and Steamer accounts — going over rental accounts — Called on Mr Munro on various matters — Engaged with Mr Ritchie about New Gardin Plans

Saturday 13

Went to office and arranged various matters with country people Went to Castle and accompanied Sir James & Lady Matheson to examine ground proposed for new Gardin which is shifted nearer the Castle in order to keep it on hard ground Mr Ritchie is to prepare plans & sound the depth of the moss — It was proposed to shift the gardin to the outer end of the meadow or to the ground prepared at the mill but both these places were thought too far from the Castle for the Gardiner to attend — Returned to the office and was engaged writing letters — Meeting with Mr Callender & Mr Gair granting orders for payment of various a/cs — going over arrears of Feu duties etc — Gave Mr Callender Mossend lease with letter from Mr Munro claiming meliorations, stated my grounds of objections & asked his advice —

Monday 15

Went to office received letters by packet — Going over lotting plans with Mr Cameron — Engaged with Mr Callender at Mr Scobie & Mr Gairs a/cs — Mr Callender has taken up the matter of the Mossend meliorations which I think he might have left to me, & attend to his own business. I merely asked his advice which need not occupy more than a few minutes of his time — Settling a/cs with various parties — Going over rentals — Reading Emigrants letters with the view of seeing which should be printed etc

Tuesday 16

Went to the office and met parties Mr Houston McLeod Valtos etc — Went to Castle and saw Sir James who arranged finally about situation of Gardin — Lease to Ken Murray Ness — etc etc Returned to office and was engaged with Mr Callender & Mr Gair at Steamer accounts which I see I must go over from July 1848   Mr Gair rendered his a/cs to Mr Callender from time to time but they did not meet to explain matters till now — Mr Gair charges salary till 1 Octr tho' the "Islay" steamer has been plying since Febry which cannot be allowed — Wrote Mr Munro about Angus Graham & Ness Millers a/c etc

Wednesday 17

Went to office and arranged various matters, met Miss Crichton and wrote Mr Munro about her account — Went to Castle to see Sir James — Meeting with Mr Callender and going over Steamer accounts — Called on Mr Munro — Writing letters for Steamer — Going over Mr Callenders notes of my accounts for 1848-49-50 which had I got sooner would have been answered before Mr Callender left — it is unsatisfactory to keep ones accounts so long without being certified —

Thursday 18

Went to office, went over John McKenzies Charter with Mr Munro — Went to Castle and accompanied Sir James & Lady Matheson to site of New Gardin, embankment & proposed Vinery & Orchard House. Contracted with Ken McLeod for embankment & alterations of Road. — Returned to office, at Uig Road a/cs — Met the Sheriff & Fiscal about alteration of Court House seating — Had call from the Banker who wished me to accompany him to the Church to see poors money divided, which I declined being much engaged — Writing letters — Settled with D. Mackenzie Dalbeg for Law business done by him which was placed to his a/c — Settled with Donald McDonald Black Smith for work done for last 6 months —

Friday 19

At office settling accounts with A McLeod for Repairs of Uig road and Kean Reasort work — With Rod^k Adam for repairs of Store Houses — With Mr McPherson Galson for meat supplied to Castle for last year etc With Thos Clark for Cattle — Had meeting with Rev^d McGrigor, the Banker — Mr Munro regarding letter to Alex McKenzie, writing letters & answers to Mr Watson objections to paying rent — engaged at office till 6 A.M. —

Saturday 20th Dec^r

At office writing letters — Contracted with Mr Houston for trenching new gardin @ £5.6/8 per acre — Went to Castle and there met Mr G McLeod Callanish, Sir James told him that his house would be made comfortable and that a deduction of his rent would be considered — That he would instruct me on the subject — Sir James refused Houston & McPherson Galson the outlay on draining applied for by them — Consulted Sir James about Gardin Wall but came to no arrangement — Returned to office and met Mr McAuley Linshader, Houston, McPherson, McLeod Valtos etc etc — Writing letters and going over accounts —

Monday 22 Dec^r

Going over Watsons corrispondence and writing him — Writing letters to various parties — meeting Mr Milbank about an addition which he wishes to make to Aline Cottage at his own expence but hopes to be allowed something for it at the end of the 7 years lease — going over and examining accts Arranging matters with Bowie — G McLeod etc — Reading over Emigrants letters with the view of seeing which should be translated

Tuesday 23 Dec^r

At office meeting Mr McAuley Linshader and Mr Cameron regarding Arinish submission Writing letters — Went to Castle saw Sir James & with him inspected the trenching of the new Gardin etc Went to Steamers office and assisted in arranging a/cs with Fairly — Fixed on situation for shed to be built on Pier by owners of the Islay Returned to office, received Packet letters and wrote answers to same — Consulted with Mr Munro about appealing against property tax and sent notice of same to the Surveyor — Arranged with Rod^k Mackenzie to audit the Lochs Poor Law boards a/cs for 21/-, gave John McKay emigrants letters to translate etc

Wednesday 24 Dec^r

Went to office and met crew of vessel shipwrecked at Uist who wished to be relieved by me as agent for the Shipwrecked Mariners Society, which I refused except in the case of one of them who is a member — gave them all an order for a passage to Glasgow & a letter to the agent there — Forwarded various claims to the Society for losses sustained by Fishermen — Met various parties & wrote letters — Met Mr John Mackenzie and accompanied him to Mr Munros office where we revised and signed dft of disposition in his favour of property purchased from Miss Crichton — also revised charter for other property purchased by him — Settled accounts with Fairly, Pope, Wm Gerrie for Uig Road etc   Meeting with Mr Hutchinson & Mr Milbank etc Writing letters for Steamer and going over Lawson & Cross's accounts for seeds, Guano etc

Thursday 25 Dec^r

At office going over the Callanish Inn Bills, settling wages with foreman of Shawbost Quay — Meeting Humphrey the tenant of Doune Caroloway who paid a portion of the stock by a contra a/c for repairs of Roads — he has as yet paid no rent and I fear never will, tho' he seems quite confident that he will make the farm pay & meet all demands — Met various Country people — Writing letters — engaged at Mr Scobies a/cs — going over Rental accounts etc

Friday 26 Dec^r

At office writing letters — made estimate for building Gardin Wall, sent offers to Sir James — Going over accounts and granting orders for payment of same — going over Mr Callenders notes on my accounts with Mr Nicolson & Mr Morison

Saturday 27

At office writing ground officers about kelp etc   Going over paybills for people working at Grounds, Home Farm etc   Called on Sir James & shewed him these bills — Remained at the Distillery all day seeing the men paid, & arranged various matters with foremen —

Monday 29th

Went to meet Mr Clark and pointed out to him site for building Haddock House. — Went to office and wrote letters, going over accounts — Meeting parties Mr Munro, Mr Hutchinson, Houston, Rigg, C. I. Nicolson who refuses to pay his store rent on the plea that he was promised if he gave satisfaction extra Salary which he did not get, he founds on a letter from Sir James which he cannot produce — I told him that if such was talked of it was altogether optional with Sir James to grant it, that his a/cs were not yet reported on by Mr Callender, and when that was done I would lay the matter before Sir James — Writing letters for Packet — Called on Mr Munro etc —

Tuesday 30th

At office going over Mr Munros a/c for Law Expences etc and comparing same with vouchers — Meeting parties — Went to the Bank and consulted the Banker on various matters — Went to Castle saw Sir James about gardiner etc — returned to office and met Mr Hutchinson about proposed let of Soval, told him that Sir James would not become bound not to fish the mouths of any of the rivers except the Black Water — Had a long conversation with the Gardiner and did all I could to get him to stay said he would think of it till morning — Settled with John McPherson for work done on his farm — Settled with Houston for his rent etc —

Wednesday 31

At office — Settled with the Gardiner for his wages — Wrote letters — going over details of return made for Property Tax. Saw Mr Munro on the subject — Went to the Castle to see Sir James he is determined to stand on the return made by him — He wishes to commence arrangements for next years emigration, but will send none but those who have land & are in arrear of rent — Is anxious to send some young men to Australia etc saw Mr Munro again & went over appeal drawn up by him against Property Tax, wrote Campbell the Surveyor and other parties by the Steamer — Wrote advertisments for Holm, Sandwick Hill & Stoneyfield — Made out bills of lading for about 20 tons kelp sent to Liverpool etc

DOCUMENTS AND ILLUSTRATIONS

The testimonial written by a local minister, Reverend John Cameron, for the Diarist as he set out in search of his first job:

That the bearer HEREOF Mr John Mackenzie lawful son of John Mackenzie Sheriff of Lewis, is a young gentleman of an amiable disposition, genteel in his manners, affable in his conversation and mild in his deportment - that he is a young man of promising talents, respectable acquirements and moral abilities - though tall he is but young and used to make a respectable appearance in his classes, & studied with persevering assiduity - that he leaves Stornoway for Glasgow with the good wishes of all his acquaintances both young and old, and that so far as is known to me, who have been acquainted with him from his infancy, he is free from the vices common to his age, being watched by paternal care and brought up by his parents in the Fear, Nurture and Admonition of the Lord and whose pious example I hope he will imitate.

All certified at Tong Manse of Stornoway, The Fourteenth Day of April Eighteen Hundred and Thirty Seven Years by me.

John Cameron,
Minister

Letter of application from John Munro Mackenzie to [*Sir*] James Matheson, applying for the post of Chamberlain.

Millbrae, Pollockshaws,
Glasgow.

25th March 1848

Sir,

Being informed that the factorship of the Lews is vacant by the retirement of Mr Scobie, I beg to offer myself as a candidate for that office.

I am a native of the Lews, my father having been for 28 years Sheriff Substitute of that district — I left the Lews nearly twelve years ago, came to Glasgow and served an apprenticeship as a Civil Engineer, where I had much practise in the construction of Works, Land and Mineral conveying etc. On the expiry of my indenture I was appointed Resident Engineer of a Railway in the neighbourhood of Glasgow (the Wishaw & Coltness). Afterwards, I became Manager as well as Engineer and then had the charge of the finance and general business of the Company, when large sums of money passed through my hands (say £50,000 per annum) and in this way I have obtained a considerable knowledge of business and accounts. Though perhaps owing more to circumstances than to anything else, I may mention that the Railway paid only a dividend of 3 per cent the year before I took charge of it, and when I left it last year (in consequence of its having been purchased by Caledonian Railway and forming a part of that Railway) it paid a dividend of $10\frac{1}{2}$ per cent. I have been for the last year employed in the construction of the Glasgow Barrhead & Neilston Railway of which I am the Resident Engineer, and have the whole works under my charge. Having been always employed in rural districts and having much intercourse with the agricultural classes in buying and settling for land, surveying etc., I have acquired a considerable knowledge of farming and improvement of land. I have had for some years past a large number of men under my charge and consequently have had some experience in the management of the working classes. I at present hold a pretty good situation here (nearly £500 per annum) and from my practical knowledge of my profession, have a good prospect before me of rising in it. However, I would prefer to assist you in the improvement of my native land, which I know you have so much at heart, but of course would not think of giving up my connections in this part of the Country without expecting a liberal remuneration.

My knowledge of Engineering would I consider be of great use in carrying on improvements in a new country, and with it I have had considerable experience in conducting general business, but as I fear I have already said too much regarding myself, I beg to refer you for further information to the following noblemen and gentlemen - viz.

The Right Honourable Lord Belhaven, Wishaw, Hamilton,
Sir Henry Seton Stewart Bart., Allantow House, Hamilton,
North Dalrymple, Cleland House, Holytown,
Charles Cowan Esq., M.P. for Edinburgh,
James Smith Esq., of Deanston, Glasgow,
Rev. Dr. McLeod, Glasgow,
Neil Robson Esq., C.E., Glasgow,
John & Walter Cum Esqs., Glasgow,
C.A. King Esq., Sec. of Caledonian Railway, Glasgow,
Alexander Glasgow, Merchant, Glasgow,
Lawrance Robertson Esq., Manager Royal Bank, Glasgow,
Graham Hutchison Esq., Merchant, Glasgow.

I could give you many more names but no doubt you will think the above quite enough. I could get letters if you prefer it to the trouble of writing the parties.

I am, Sir,
Your most obedient servant,
J. MUNRO MACKENZIE

James Matheson Esq., M.P.

P.S. Though I am a native of Lews, I have no near relatives there with the exception of my mother and aunts.

The Diarist is shown (arrowed) in this section of a painting commissioned to commemorate the laying of the foundation stone of Lews Castle. Also shown in the foreground are his employer, Sir James Matheson and Lady Matheson. Others who are mentioned in the *Diary* may be identified from the key to the painting on pages 160/161. It may be noted that John Munro Mackenzie's predecessor, John Scobie, is shown standing beside him, and described in the key as Chamberlain. It seems fair to assume, however, that by the time the painting was completed, John Munro Mackenzie had succeeded to the post and was therefore included.

Photo by R. Alastair Barr

The painting hangs in the Masonic Lodge and is reproduced here by kind permission of Lodge Fortrose No. 108, Stornoway.

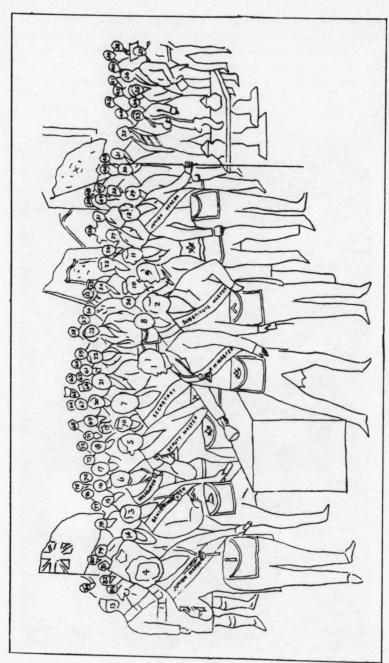

KEY TO THE MASONIC PICTURE.

List of Names in Key to Masonic Picture.

1 Roderick Morrison, Banker......R.W.M.
2 James Robertson McIver, of Gress S.M.
3 Daniel Lewis McKenzie, Shipowner. S.W.
4 John Furse, Supervisor of Inland
    Revenue...................... J.W.
5 Norman McIver, Banker, ... D.M.
6 Colin Morrison, Merchant .... Treas.
7 Roderick McKenzie, Town Clerk, Secy.
8 Donald Beaton, Tailor .... Tyler.
9 John McAulay, Merchant .... P.M.
10 Malcolm McAulay, Merchant ....
11 John McKenzie, Contractor, Bible Bearer
12 John White, Inland Revenue .... J.D.
13 Thomas McKay, Piper.
14 Rev. John Macrae, E. C. Minister.
15 Hugh Suter, Mason.
16 Alexander Gair, Mason.
17 John McKenzie, Shipmaster.
18 James Christie, Mason.
19 David Rae, Painter.
20 Dr. A. McIver.
21 John McLeod, of Hudson's Bay.
22 ——— McDonald.
23 John Reid McKenzie, Shipowner.
24 Chas. Wilson, Architect.
25 Hugh Brown, Jailer.
26 Thomas Clark, Baker.
27 Capt. Neil Morrison, R. N.
28 Donald Munro, Procurator Fiscal.
29 Daniel Murray, Tidewaiter.
30 Capt. R. T. Hudson, Hutchinson's Stmrs.
31 Roderick Nicholson, Shipowner.
32 Sir James Matheson, Prop. of the Lews.
33 Lady Matheson.
34 Mrs. Watt.
35 Capt. Benjamin Oliver.
36 Sheriff Substitute Andrew McDonald.
37 Capt. Richard Burnaby, R. S. & M.
38 Robt. Grant Massou, the Artist.
39 Charles Howitt, Architect.
40 James Perrie, Solicitor.
41 J. Munro McKenzie.
42 John Scobie, Chamberlain.
43 Kennenh Morrison, Flesher.
44 Rev. Geo. Shipton.
45 Master David McDonald.
46 Master Duncan McKenzie.
47 John Urquhart, Painter.
48 William McKay.
49 John McAlpine, P.M.
50 Donald McKenzie, Shipmaster.
51 Robert Pritchard, Teacher.
52 Corporal James Kielle, R. S. & M.
53 Donald Morrison, Seaman.
54 A. T. Chatfield, Compt. of Customs.
55 John Rae, Shipwright.
56 Archibald McLellan, "Mary Jane."
57 David Corner, Fishery Officer.
58 Alexander McKenzie, Joiner.
59 Alexander McLean, Ship Carpenter.
60 Murdo Lead, Baker.
61 Roderick Millar, Surgeon.
62 Mrs. McLeod, Belleville.
63 Donald Matheson, R. S. & M.
64 Roderick McKay, Gamekeeper.
65 Henry Stafford, R. S. & M.
66 William Auckburn, R. S, & M.
67 Duncan Grant, Bookseller,
68 John Munro, Excise Officer.
69 Revd. Mr. Watson, Uig.
70 Peter McNab, Carting Contractor.
71 Roderick Nicholson Junr., now of Tigh-
    nabruaich.
72 McEachan, Steward of Steamer.
73 Colin John Nicholson, Clerk.
74 Alex. Robertson, Shipowner.
75 Angus Mckay, Supt. Herring Fishery.
76 Robert Wilson, Gas Manager.
77 Murdo McKenzie, Shipowner.
78 Alexander Morrison.
79 W. T. Jeffries, Collector of Customs.
80 Alexander McKenzie, Architect.
81 Hugh McPherson, Galson.
82 Hugh McLachlan, Merchant.
83 Murdo McIver.
84 James Robertson, C. E.

From *Annals of Lodge Fortrose No. 108, Stornoway, 1767-1905*. Compiled from the Lodge records by J. Campbell Smith B. Sc. (Printed 1905)

1. 112 families have volunteered to emigrate this season 184 families have been told that they may avail themselves of the proposed means of emigration which latter number are on an average upwards of £10. in arrear of Rent and the greater number of whom have not any visible means for their support till next crop

2. It is proposed that the emigrants shall embark during the month of may 1851 either at Stornoway of Loch Roag as may be arranged; a free passage and food during the voyage being secured to them

3. The locality fixed on as their destination is Qubec in the first place from whence they will be forwarded to the Eastern Townships of Lower Canada, or Montreal in their option

4. On arrival at Qubec the ordinary Govt. Tax or Head money will be paid by the party sending the Emigrants and for which Tax the Government Emigration Agent will forward them from Qubec to the above localities where employment and land can be procured.

5. By the summonses of removal executed it cannot be inferred that compulsory emigration is in contemplation
   The execution of these writs apply to the second class of tenants mentioned in the first Query being parties who are entirely destitute of the means of supporting themselves till next crop. many of whom have not

at present seed to lay down a crop. far less the means or prospect of paying their arrears or current rents; they also apply to persons who are supposed to be able but unwilling to pay their rents, while at the same time they are in no way respect in as good circumstances as those Tenants who are not in arrears of Rent. Both of these classes of Tenants have it in their option to emigrate to a country where by industry and perseverance they can be more comfortable than here and freed from their present diffi:-culties by the Proprietor relinquishing all claims to arrears of Rent and giving them full value for such stock as they have for disposal, for the purpose of providing clothing and securing a fund to meet emergencies. The system of daily increasing arrears has an evident immoral tendency upon the industrious and well paying class of Tenants, while if no difference is made in the treatment of those who endeavour to pay and those who make no effort to pay there is no encouragement held out to the sober and industrious

6. It is intended to engage and send a Minister or Teacher with the emigrants and the Free Church Presbytery have it in their power to recommend a fit person to watch over the spiritual and social interests of these emigrants

Lews Castle; the home of Sir James and Lady Matheson and focus for much of John Munro Mackenzie's daily routine

When John Munro Mackenzie and his family left Lewis in 1854 the contents of his home
— Sandwick Cottage in Stornoway — were sold by public auction:

SALE OF

HOUSEHOLD FURNITURE, FARM STOCK & IMPLEMENTS

There will be Sold by PUBLIC AUCTION, at

SANDWICK COTTAGE, STORNOWAY,

On THURSDAY, 25th May, and Day Following;

The Whole Household Furniture, Farm Stock and Implements, belonging to Mr. J. M. MACKENZIE,
as under :—viz.

DINING-ROOM.

Mahogany Sideboard.
Do.   Set of Dining Tables on Pillar and Claw.
Do.   Set of 12 Chairs, and Sofa in Haircloth.
Rosewood Spirit Case.
Carpet and Rug.
Fender and Fire Irons.
5 Coloured Engravings, Framed.
Moreen Window Curtains and Cornice.
Mahogany Dining Table on Pillar and Claw.
8 Maple Chairs in Haircloth.
2 Spoon Boxes.   Plate Warmer.

DRAWING-ROOM.

Rosewood Centre Table.
Do.   Cabinet.
Do.   Couch covered in Drab Damask.
Do.   Easy Chair   do.   do.
Do.   Chairs.
Do.   Imitation, Fancy Chairs.
Do.   Devotional Chair.
2 Oakroot Card Tables.
Work Table, Maple.
2 Gilt Window Cornices.
2 Sets Drab Damask Window Curtains.
Brussels Carpet and Rug.
Mahogany Spring Bottom Couch covered with Chintz.
8 Imitation Rosewood Chairs with Mixed Damask and
      Chintz Covers.
Eight-Day Time Piece.
Pictures.

WEST FRONT BEDROOM.

Mahogany French Bedstead.
Do.   Chest of Drawers.
Do.   Toilet Table, and 1 Hardwood do.
Do.   Toilet Glasses.
Do.   Wash-Hand Stand, containing Stool and Bath.
Do.   Towel Screen.
5 Cane Chairs.
Bedroom Ware.
Carpet and Rug.
Fender and Fire Irons.

EAST FRONT BEDROOM.

Hardwood French Bedstead.
Do.   Chest of Drawers with Wardrobe.
2 Do.   Toilet Tables.
2 Do.   Toilet Glasses.
Ottoman, which will make into a Bed or Easy Chair.
Towel Screen and Wash-Hand Stand.
Carpet and Rug.
Fender and Fire Irons.
Bedroom Ware.

WEST BACK BEDROOM

2 French Bedsteads.
Mahogany Chest of Drawers.
Toilet Table.
Toilet Glass.
Wash-Hand Stand.
Bedroom Ware.
Chairs.
Carpet and Rug.
Fender and Fire Irons.

EAST BEDROOM.

EAST BEDROOM—*Continued.*

2 Dressing Glasses.
Cane Chairs.
Bedroom Ward.
Carpet and Fender.

NURSERY.

Iron Bedstead.
2 Oak Children's Cribs.
Chest of Drawers.
Folding Table.
Chairs.
Fender.

KITCHEN.

Dresser.
Tables.
Chairs.
Stools.
Cooking Utensils.

PANTRY.

Glass Tumblers.
Wine Glasses.
Wine Decanters.
Staffordshire China Dinner Set, complete.
White and Gold China Breakfast Set.
Tea Trays.
Small do.
Set of 8 Britannia Metal Dish Covers.
Japanned Tea Kettle with Stand.
Breakfast Tea Kettle.

PARLOUR IN COTTAGE.

Set of Mahogany Dining Tables.
12   do.   Chairs in Haircloth.
Stuffed Sofa with Moreen and Chintz Cover.
Carpet and Rug.
Fender and Fire Irons.

LOBBY AND STAIRS.

Mahogany Hall Table.
do.   Chairs.
Cocoa Mat.
Door Mats.
Pieces Stair Carpeting.
Spring Candle Lamp.
Eight-Day Clock.

KITCHEN IN COTTAGE.

Dresser.
Table.
Chairs.
Stools.
Press Bed.
Meat Safe.
Wire Covers.

FARM STOCK AND IMPLEMENTS.

			£	s	d
6 Ayrshire Milch Cows.			50	5	
2 do. Queys.			55	14	
Draught Mare.			25	5	
2 Ponies.			78	7	
Plough.			13	5	
Pair Harrows.			7	10	
			2	6	

165

Family tree

John Munro Mackenzie, the Diarist, was a descendant of Alexander "Ionraic" Mackenzie, VII Baron of Kintail (d. 1488) through the family connection of Gairloch and then of Letterewe, as shown in this relevant (and simplified) portion of the family tree:

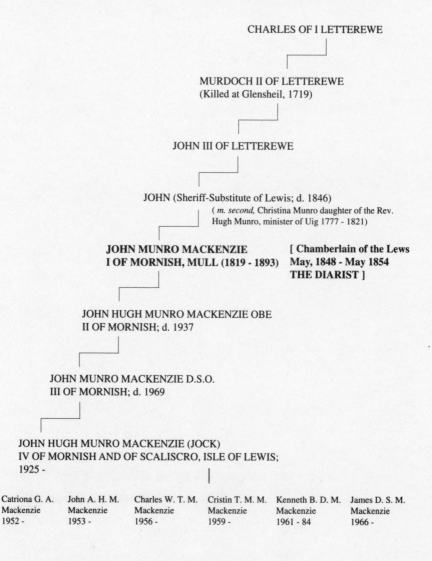

CHARLES OF I LETTEREWE

MURDOCH II OF LETTEREWE
(Killed at Glensheil, 1719)

JOHN III OF LETTEREWE

JOHN (Sheriff-Substitute of Lewis; d. 1846)
(*m. second,* Christina Munro daughter of the Rev.
Hugh Munro, minister of Uig 1777 - 1821)

JOHN MUNRO MACKENZIE   **[Chamberlain of the Lews**
I OF MORNISH, MULL (1819 - 1893)   **May, 1848 - May 1854**
   THE DIARIST]

JOHN HUGH MUNRO MACKENZIE OBE
II OF MORNISH; d. 1937

JOHN MUNRO MACKENZIE D.S.O.
III OF MORNISH; d. 1969

JOHN HUGH MUNRO MACKENZIE (JOCK)
IV OF MORNISH AND OF SCALISCRO, ISLE OF LEWIS;
1925 -

Catriona G. A.	John A. H. M.	Charles W. T. M.	Cristin T. M. M.	Kenneth B. D. M.	James D. S. M.
Mackenzie	Mackenzie	Mackenzie	Mackenzie	Mackenzie	Mackenzie
1952 -	1953 -	1956 -	1959 -	1961 - 84	1966 -